Creative Writing

If you want to know how...

Handbook for Writers of English
Punctuation, common practice and usage

Practical Research Methods
Up-to-date ways to master research in six stages

Writing Your Life Story
How to record and present your memories
for future generations to enjoy

Touch Typing in 10 Hours
Gain a valuable skill that will last a lifetime

Quick Solutions to Common Errors in English
An A–Z guide to spelling, punctuation and grammar

howtobooks

Please send for a free copy of the latest catalogue:

How To Books
3 Newtec Place, Magdalen Road,
Oxford OX4 1RE, United Kingdom
email: info@howtobooks.co.uk
http://www.howtobooks.co.uk

Creative Writing

How to unlock your
imagination, develop
your writing skills –
and get published

Adèle Ramet

REVISED AND UPDATED 5TH EDITION

howtobooks

Published by How To Books Ltd,
3 Newtec Place, Magdalen Road,
Oxford OX4 1RE. United Kingdom.
Tel: (01865) 793806. Fax: (01865) 248780.
email: info@howtobooks.co.uk
www.howtobooks.co.uk

First published 1997
Second edition 1999
Third edition 2001
Fourth edition 2003
Fifth edition 2004

British Library Cataloguing in Publication Data
A catalogue record for this book is available from
the British Library

Cartoons by Simon Ramet
Cover design by Baseline Arts Ltd, Oxford

Produced for How To Books by Deer Park Productions,
Tavistock
Typeset by PDQ Typesetting, Newcastle-under-Lyme, Staffs
Printed and bound by The Cromwell Press, Trowbridge,
Wiltshire

NOTE: The material contained in this book is set out in good
faith for general guidance and no liability can be accepted
for loss or expense incurred as a result of relying in particular
circumstances on statements made in the book. Laws and
regulations are complex and liable to change, and readers should
check the current position with the relevant authorities before
making personal arrangements.

Contents

List of illustrations

Preface

WHAT IS CREATIVE WRITING?

The popular perception of the term 'creative writer' can be misleading. To some, it conjures up a lofty, arty image. To others, it implies amateur status. A creative writer is, we feel, somehow different from those published professionals whose words we so avidly read in newspapers, magazines and books.

In fact, creative writers come in all shapes, sizes, ages and from all walks of life and their writing covers a diverse range of interests.

So, what is creative writing? *Chambers Dictionary* defines **creative** as 'Having the power to create, that creates, showing, pertaining to, imagination, originality' and **writing** as 'The act of one who writes, that which is written, literary production or composition'. Therefore, the term 'creative writing' may be defined as:

**Having the power to create an imaginative,
original literary production or composition**

and can be applied to a very broad spectrum of writing genres.

In this book we will be looking at:

- ways of drawing on personal experience in order to write non-fiction articles on a wide variety of topics in a number of different styles

◆ fiction writing and the world of genre fiction – science, romance, horror and crime

◆ writing for children which requires specialised skills that, once mastered, bring enormous satisfaction to both the writer and the reader.

Finally, there will be advice and guidance on how to turn your writing into a marketable commodity for, even though many people set out to write purely for their own pleasure, there is little doubt that nothing can compare to the thrill of having work accepted for publication and reading it from a printed page.

AUTHOR'S NOTE

I would like to thank authors **Patricia Burns**, **Martina Cole**, **Jonathan Gash**, **Michael Green**, **Susan Moody**, **Margaret Nash** and **Ruth Rendell**, agents **Carole Blake** of Blake Friedmann, **Peters Fraser & Dunlop** and editors **Richard Bell** of *Writers News* and **Harcourt Education Ltd.** for their invaluable contributions to this book.

ACKNOWLEDGEMENTS

The Art of Coarse Sailing, Michael Green, Arrow Books.
Cinnamon Alley, Patricia Burns, Century Arrow.
Hush-a-Bye, Susan Moody, Hodder & Stoughton.
The Judas Pair, Jonathan Gash, Collins/Viking Penguin.
Some Lie and Some Die, Ruth Rendell, Arrow Books.
The Ladykiller, Martina Cole, Hodder Headline.

Adèle Ramet

$$\left(1 \right)$$

Getting Started

MAKING TIME TO WRITE

One of the first rules to remember is that writers write. You should write something every day, even if all you do with the finished piece is tear it up and throw it away.

Writing something, anything, every day will enable you to build up the discipline and commitment required to ensure that you can produce a complete manuscript in whatever genre you choose.

Giving yourself permission to write

Due to a common misconception that unless you are a published novelist, you cannot be considered a 'real' writer, novice authors often find it difficult to convince either their nearest and dearest or, indeed, themselves that their desire to write should be taken seriously.

However, even the most famous authors had to start somewhere, so don't be put off by outside pressures. Be assured that your writing is more important than:

- mowing the lawn
- washing the dishes
- cleaning, dusting, gardening

or any other similar activity that will keep you from your pen and paper.

Locking the door

One successful Mills & Boon author states that, once she had made up her mind to become a novelist, she turned one room of her house into a study, locked the door and forbade anyone to enter whilst she was working.

You may not feel you have to go quite this far but it is important to set aside both a space in your home where you can work and make a regular time to write.

Making time

Lack of time is, perhaps, the most commonly used excuse for not putting pen to paper. This can be justified with a number of perfectly credible explanations:

- You have a demanding full-time job.
- You have a large family.
- You have to get those seedlings planted.
- You have too many other commitments.
- You're too tired.

Perhaps all these excuses can be rolled into one simple explanation:

- **You don't think you're good enough.**

Building confidence

Lack of confidence is a major stumbling block for the would-be writer. There is no easy way round this but if you really want to write, the only option is to get on and do it. Taking the following steps can help:

- Set aside a corner in your home solely for your writing.

- Keep a notebook in which to jot down ideas.

- Select a suitable time to write each day and stick to it.

- Give yourself a time limit for writing, say, an hour a day to begin with.

- Write something every day and even if you think it's terrible, retain it until the next day.

- Begin by re-reading what you wrote yesterday; at the very least it will encourage you to rewrite. At best, it will be much better than you thought and spur you on to write more.

- Buy a good dictionary and thesaurus.

- Manuscripts intended for publication must be typewritten so, if possible, use a personal computer (PC). The more professional your writing looks, the more professional you will feel.

WHERE DO YOU GET YOUR IDEAS?

Having made the decision to write, the next step is finding something to write about.

Watching the world go by

Watch how people behave in everyday situations, jotting down ideas in your notebook as they occur to you.

The next time you go to the supermarket, for example, observe the behaviour of the other customers. Take a few seconds to chat to the checkout girl or the assistant who packs your shopping. Listen not only to the words they say but to how they say them.

If you commute to work, use your journey time to study your fellow travellers. Try to imagine what sort of homes they come from and how they might lead their lives. Whatever situation you find yourself in during your daily life, observe the people around you.

Not only should you watch but you must also listen. Writers are terrible eavesdroppers and will shamelessly listen in on the most private conversations. You can pick up some wonderful snippets that will effortlessly turn themselves into ideas for all sorts of things, from brief letters to your favourite magazine, factual articles explaining the apparently inexplicable, to lengthy works of fiction.

Keeping an eye on the media

Perhaps the richest sources of ideas are newspapers, television and radio. Keep your eyes and ears open for the unusual stories and quirky programmes tucked away between the major items. All kinds of things can capture your imagination.

Not so long ago, a BBC Radio 4 programme about the potentially dull topic of making a will inspired me to write a short story for *Bella* magazine's 'Mini Mystery' page. The programme highlighted the legal pitfalls facing people who wish to make unusual wills and the idea captured my imagination.

Having gleaned the necessary technical legal information, I soon had the protagonist, beneficiary and terms of the will clearly formed in my mind. From there, it was a short step to writing the story, sending it off to my editor and seeing it in print.

Sources of ideas

Ideas are all around you, if only you can train yourself to find them. Listed below are just a few possible sources:

- airports
- beaches
- buses, coaches, planes and trains
- cafés and restaurants
- clubs
- doctors'/dentists' surgeries
- hairdressers
- school playgrounds
- shops
- stations.

The list is endless but as a general rule, ideas are to be found anywhere a number of people gather in one place.

WRITING AURALLY AND VISUALLY

Having developed your watching and listening skills, it can nevertheless be quite difficult to set them down on paper. More often than not, a phrase that sounded wonderful in your head looks dull and lifeless when it hits the page.

Later in the book, we will be looking at ways of bringing your writing to life and obtaining that vital ingredient, reader identification. You will learn how to stimulate the reader's senses so that they identify with the people being portrayed, see and hear the sights and sounds you are attempting to convey.

Long descriptive passages, no matter how beautifully written, can be very dull without dialogue, action or interaction to liven them up. People enjoy reading about people, so even the most factual non-fiction article can be enriched by the inclusion of a brief interview with an acknowledged expert or a comment from someone involved in the featured topic.

For fiction, too, there is no better way to convey setting, atmosphere, sights, sounds and scents than through the reactions of your characters.

Whatever genre you choose, be sure you know the true meaning of each word you use, consulting your dictionary and thesaurus whenever you are unsure about the spelling or context of a word or phrase.

DRAWING ON YOUR OWN EXPERIENCES

One of the first rules a would-be writer learns is to '**write about what you know**'. If, however, this rule is taken too literally, few writers would ever gain the requisite knowledge to write an historical romance, murder mystery or science fiction novel.

Far more practical is the advice from bestselling author Martina Cole to '**Write about what you know and if you don't know – find out**'.

You don't need to have lived in a previous century, be a murderer or travel in space to write genre fiction. Thorough research into the background against which your story is set should provide you with the factual information you require.

Expert knowledge is invaluable, of course. Years spent in industry or in the legal, nursing or teaching profession; seeing active service in the armed forces; bringing up a family on a low fixed income; working long shifts on a factory assembly line; running and perhaps losing your own business – any one of these and similar experiences offers a wealth of information on which you can draw, but factual accuracy is only one aspect of writing. You also have to find a way to breathe life into the characters featured in your articles and stories and this comes from your experience of personal relationships, both good and bad.

From our earliest memories of childhood through our school-days to adult friendships, romantic attachments, experiences at work and in our domestic lives, everything that went into forming our character has a part to play in our writing.

LOOKING BACK INTO YOUR PAST

There is little doubt that anyone with a chequered past will have plenty to write about but many of us feel we have done very little in our lives worth committing to paper.

On closer inspection, however, this is very rarely the case. Take yourself right back to your earliest memories. How did you feel when:

- you were told off for being naughty?
- you were picked on by other children?
- you missed out on a treat?
- your parents argued?
- you got detention at school?
- you had to have treatment in hospital?
- a family trauma made you realise that nothing at home would be the same again?

These are just a few experiences many children share, but try going up a notch in age and see if you can recall how you felt when:

- you left home
- started your first day at work
- travelled abroad on your own
- got your first cheque book
- bought your own car.

Seeking reader identification

By now, you may be wondering how such very ordinary, everyday experiences can possibly be relevant to creative writing. Surely writing is all about escapism, original ideas, unusual situations, not about opening a 'Young Saver' bank account?

Of course, you're right. Originality is a vital ingredient in any piece of writing, fact or fiction, but then so is realism. Without realism, you cannot have reader identification and it is this element that brings your work vividly to life.

Observing everyday life

Michael Green, professional journalist and author of many humorous non-fiction books, offers the following excellent advice to would-be writers:

> *'Observe everyday life with a writer's eye. There lies your material. Carry a notebook and jot down any ideas that come or incidents you can see.'*

READ, READ, READ

Whatever your writing interest may be, fiction or non-fiction, literary novels or specialist articles, you should read anything and everything in your chosen genre.

Reading with a writer's eye

This book is designed to help you understand how to read with a writer's eye, taking the time to analyse how an author manages to grab your attention and hold it so that you keep on reading through to the end.

Your notebook will become a valuable source of reference. Failure to write ideas down can result in you losing them altogether. Committing them to paper helps commit them to memory and stimulate new writing projects.

Use the questionnaire in Figure 1 to analyse published examples of your particular writing interest. Whether you intend to write non-fiction articles, short stories or novels, you will discover that the same basic principles apply.

As your critical faculties develop, you may find your reading enjoyment is spoilt by the way technical points you were previously unaware of suddenly become glaringly obvious.

The following questions are designed to provide an insight into the techniques employed by published authors of both fact and fiction to catch and hold their readers' attention.

		Yes	No
1.	Was the first sentence shorter than the others in the opening paragraph?	☐	☐
2.	Was the first paragraph shorter than the second?	☐	☐
3.	Did the first paragraph tell you what the article/story was about?	☐	☐
4.	What was it about the article/story that made you read on?		
	(a) You wanted to know how to perform a specific task	☐	☐
	(b) You found the topic fascinating	☐	☐
	(c) You discovered something you didn't know before	☐	☐
	(d) You had to know what happened next	☐	☐
	(e) You wanted to find out how it all ended	☐	☐
5.	Was the middle informative/entertaining?	☐	☐
6.	Was it set out in a logical order?	☐	☐
7.	Did each section/scene lead you on to read the next?	☐	☐
8.	Did you feel compelled to keep reading?	☐	☐
9.	If characters were included, could you relate to them?	☐	☐
10.	Did the end bring the whole thing to a logical conclusion?	☐	☐
11.	Was the ending satisfactory?	☐	☐
12.	Were all the questions answered/loose ends tied up?	☐	☐
13.	Did the author deliver what they promised?	☐	☐
14.	Did you enjoy reading it?	☐	☐
15.	Would you read more by this author?	☐	☐

Answers to the above questions should mostly be 'Yes'.

Fig. 1. Analysis sheet.

Gradually, however, as your new-found understanding helps you to appreciate the skills being employed, the sheer pleasure of reading something that is both beautifully written and well-constructed will return and increase.

By the time this stage is reached, your own writing will be showing a marked improvement.

CHECKLIST

1. Have you set aside a corner of your home where you can write?

2. Have you established a set time of day just for writing?

3. Do you keep a notebook of ideas?

4. Do you write something every day?

5. Do you read extensively?

6. Have you decided what you want to write about?

ASSIGNMENT

Take your notebook and jot down 10 ideas for articles or stories. By the time you have finished reading this book, you should have developed at least one of those ideas into a workable outline.

2

Writing Non-Fiction

WRITING ABOUT WHAT YOU KNOW

As we saw in the previous chapter, one of the first pieces of advice any would-be writer learns is to write about what you know.

This can be interpreted as anything from factual articles about a hobby, profession or skill to writing your life-story. You can be sure that everyone has experience in one area or another that will be of interest to someone else.

LETTING OFF STEAM

For the avid newspaper and magazine reader, the temptation to write a learned piece complaining about the state of the nation or the rising price of a pack of frozen peas can be overwhelming.

It is tempting to try to emulate controversial comment columns in the hope that a discerning editor will be keen to give pride of place to our words of wisdom. Sadly, this is rarely the case.

Sending letters to editors

Comment columns are usually written by staff writers, well-known journalists or political analysts. These are the professionals considered by the media to be qualified to comment on 'life, the universe and everything'.

However, as the infamous 'Disgusted of Tunbridge Wells' discovered, there is an outlet for the man or woman in the street to voice their opinion and that is through the readers' letters page.

Sending letters to editors

The letters page in any publication is an excellent way of letting off steam in print. It can also be a way of earning small amounts of cash or gifts for your writing.

If you like the idea of making your voice heard, you stand a better chance of having a letter published if you follow a few simple rules:

♦ Write clearly and neatly or, if possible, type your letter.

♦ Address it to the correct person.

♦ Keep it brief and to the point.

♦ Make it as topical as possible.

♦ Write about something relevant to the publication's readership.

♦ A brief word of praise for the publication always helps.

♦ Invite comments or advice from other readers.

♦ **Never** send the same letter to more than one magazine at the same time. These pages operate on the assumption that all letters are from regular readers of their publication.

CHANGING WORK INTO LEISURE

There are literally hundreds of magazine titles listed in trade directories, a large proportion of which potentially offer opportunities for non-fiction writers.

Knowing your subject

Just a few of the categories into which these magazines fall are listed below:

- animals and pets
- arts and entertainment
- business and finance
- computers
- general interest
- hobbies
- home
- motoring
- music
- sports
- trade and professional
- transport
- women's interests.

Even more opportunities for would-be columnists can be found in local interest publications, parish magazines, local newspapers, club magazines etc.

Becoming a 'stringer'

If you regularly write to the letters page of a newspaper or county magazine about items of importance to the residents in your area, you may be contacted and asked if you will become a 'stringer'. This involves keeping an eye out for snippets of news and views on local issues and phoning them in to the editor.

Many regular columnists in specialist magazines begin their writing careers in this way before graduating to their own regular column.

Experts who can express themselves clearly and be relied upon to produce manuscripts on demand are few and far between. Specialist magazines and small local newspapers can offer a wonderful opportunity to pursue your writing interest by sharing information with other readers.

Constructing an article

Writing about something you enjoy can be a real labour of love. If you have the ability to impart your enthusiasm and expertise to a like-minded reader, your pleasure will be increased immeasurably by seeing your words on the pages of your favourite magazine.

Constructing a readable article is, however, not as easy as it looks. First you must study your chosen magazine and familiarise yourself with the length and style of their articles. Your opening sentence should give a clear indication of what the article is about and once you begin writing, keep to the point and don't get sidetracked.

If, for example, you are a recognised connoisseur of real ales and you want to explain how to assess a prize-winning pint, you might open the article with something along the following lines:

> With the growth in popularity of real ale, brewers are becoming highly competitive. Brewing a prize-winning pint takes skill and dedication but by following a few basic guidelines, you can find yourself up there with the front runners.

Anyone reading the article would be in no doubt as to its content and having caught their attention, you now hold it by taking them step by step through the promised guidelines.

Your closing paragraph should bring the article neatly back to the beginning, finishing with something like:

Follow these few principles and before long, your ale will take its place on the list of home-produced, award-winning real ales.

You could add to this a list of competitions and national events open to real ale brewers and drinkers but very little more would be needed other than some captioned photographs to illustrate the piece.

A simple framework of an article is set out in Figure 2. The main constituents are:

◆ a good, attention-grabbing introduction

◆ a middle, arranged in a logical order, which keeps to the subject and delivers the information promised in the introduction

♦ an ending which rounds the article off, bringing it logically back to the beginning.

INTRODUCTION (Beginning)	Introduce the subject, go straight to the point, e.g.: 'With the growth in popularity of real ale....'
CONTENT (Middle)	Keep to the point of the article, dealing with each relevant item in a logical order, e.g.: ♦ How to assess the quality, i.e. 'Points to look for...' ♦ Tips for brewing your own prize-winning ales. ♦ List of quality brews. ♦ Where to find good ales.
END	Round off article by bringing it back to the beginning, e.g. 'Follow the basic principles and before long, your ale will take its place on the list of home-produced award-winning real ales.'

Fig. 2. Framework for article.

Ideally, your opening sentence should be shorter than all the rest and should grab the reader's attention by immediately telling them what the article is about. The more technical the magazine, the more factual your article should be.

Illustrations in the form of colour slides, photographs or diagrams are always useful. These should be sensibly captioned, so that it is clear what section of the text they relate to, something like:

A judge samples my latest brew.

Expanding your idea

From one article idea can spring several more. Perhaps you could follow up the first article with an interview with a brewer and this in turn might lead to a visit to a beer festival and yet another article about that. Before long, you could find yourself becoming a regular contributor to a whole range of magazines.

RELATING YOUR LIFE-STORY

One popular non-fiction topic creative writers like to embark upon is their autobiography.

Almost everyone has a tale to tell, many of which are fascinating, even verging on the unbelievable. Those who have lived through some pretty amazing experiences understandably want to write them down, both for their own personal satisfaction and to provide a written record for future generations.

Examining your motivation

Before you begin to write your life-story, however, it is worth examining exactly what your motives are, so ask yourself the following questions:

1. Do I have a fascinating tale to tell?

2. Is my story unique?

3. Do I need to confront my past in order to move on in my life?

4. Do I wish to leave my family a record of my life?

5. Do I want to give hope to others?

6. Do I want to have my autobiography published?

Being famous

If the answer to question 6 is 'yes' the next question has to be 'Am I famous?' Unfortunately, if you're not, then the chances of having your book accepted by a publisher are very slim indeed.

The fact is that the majority of autobiographical books being published at the moment feature celebrities currently in the news, be they supermodels in their early twenties, sporting personalities, leading politicians or famous names from the world of film and television.

Compared to yours, their lives may have been extremely dull before they were propelled into the public eye but it's the here and now that matters and in today's throwaway media, fame is everything.

Informing the public

Many successful autobiographies do more than tell the author's life-story. They also provide a documentary record of historical incidents and procedures which may have been hidden from the public eye.

An autobiography which performs any one of the following functions might well be of interest to an appropriate publisher.

◆ Describes a practice which has been concealed from the public, e.g. sending orphanage children to Australia.

◆ Details the author's recovery from a potentially life-threatening illness or condition.

- Is an account of the author's experiences as a hostage, either political or during a crime.

- Tells the story of a kidnap or hijack victim.

- Gives information about a turning point in the author's life to which others can relate, e.g. nursing a disabled child.

- Details the sequence of events which led to the author setting up an international charitable organisation.

Providing a family record

For many creative writers, the sole motivation for writing their autobiography is to provide a family record for future generations.

A written record will be enhanced by the inclusion of captioned family photographs and thanks to the growth of desktop publishing, on payment of a relatively small amount, you can have your family history professionally printed and bound. This will ensure that all the information is kept together and is presented in an attractive, user-friendly way.

Shop around in the writing press to obtain several quotes from reputable sources but don't be tempted to stray into the realms of vanity publishing. These organisations, purporting to offer a publishing service to authors, can charge several hundred or even thousands of pounds for a volume which would cost a reputable printer a fraction of the price to produce.

We will be looking at vanity publishing later in the book but if you are in any doubt about the authenticity of a publisher, remember the writer's golden rule:

YOU NEVER PAY PUBLISHERS – THEY PAY YOU

For a detailed listing of reputable book and magazine publishers, see *The Writers and Artists Yearbook* (published by A & C Black).

Fictionalising the truth
Researching and writing your autobiography can prove therapeutic in more ways than one.

For many, it is a way of exorcising traumatic events, confronting their feelings and working their way through bitter experiences. It can also provide a wealth of material for a fictional novel.

Whilst a publisher is unlikely to consider the true story of a so-called 'ordinary' person, fictionalising your extraordinary life offers a more viable route to seeing your work in print.

Changing the names
If you do decide to turn your autobiography into a work of fiction, the names of your characters and their locations should be fictional too.

You may also need to alter the facts in order to make the whole thing more believable. Even though a sequence of events actually happened it can appear to be extremely unlikely. If this is true of your life-story bear in mind that, whilst truth is often stranger than fiction, for the purposes of publication, fiction has to make sense.

TELLING TRAVELLERS' TALES

For many of us, travel writing involves keeping a diary and photograph album as a pleasurable reminder of our holidays to enjoy during long winter evenings at home. Writing articles about your travels with a view to publication needs a very different approach.

Passing on information

The majority of travel features are written by professional staff writers or compiled by travel editors.

Some magazines include small snippets of information about specialist breaks. These are usually confined to details of family fun days, singles or economy breaks and these sections offer the best publishing opportunity for new writers.

Wishing you weren't here

One of the biggest problems facing the would-be travel writer is understanding the requirements of the travel industry and the tourist policy of the country they will, by their article, be promoting.

A good travel article should not be a blow by blow account of your particular holiday, nor your reactions to the people you met and the places you visited. Nor is it an opportunity for you to relate your tale of woe about the appalling journey you suffered in order to reach a half-built hotel, miles from the nearest beach.

Taking a free trip

Magazines use travel articles to inform their readers about holidays which will best suit them, so some of the points that should be included are:

- where to stay

- whether the location is suitable for families

- the safety of the beaches

- facilities available

- whether it is noisy or quiet

- what sort of nightlife it offers

- what the food is like, cost and availability

- places to visit and their accessibility in relation to the resort

- how to get there – a choice of methods is useful

- the cost of travel and accommodation – again, a selection should be given.

Whilst professional travel writers receive 'free' trips from tourist boards and travel companies, these are in return for guaranteed coverage in well-known publications, so the writer must be able to fulfil the following criteria:

- They must be prepared to follow a set itinerary.

- Publication for articles must be guaranteed in at least one reputable magazine.

- Any articles must include the features specified by the sponsoring company.

- Articles must be published to coincide with specific publicity drives.

Without some kind of a track record as a freelance article writer, it is unlikely that you would be invited by any travel company to take a free trip.

Travelling light

Travel books are a very different kettle of fish. They range from guidebooks produced by tourist boards to exciting tales of daring-do.

The intrepid traveller who crosses deserts, scales mountains and shoots rapids equipped with little more than a change of underwear, a toothbrush and a blunt penknife will clearly have a fascinating tale to tell.

It is, however, worth bearing in mind that, more often than not, our canny explorer already has a publishing contract signed and sealed before the toe of his or her walking boot hits the floor of the departure lounge at Heathrow airport.

Playing safe

Between the two ends of the scale, the standard guidebook and the one-off adventure, there is an incredibly wide range of topics for the seasoned traveller to write about. Listed below are just a few suggestions:

- handy hints on packing
- travelling throughout pregnancy and with a baby
- value family fun days out
- holidays on a budget
- backpackers' guides to a range of countries (series)

- travelling alone

- locations off the beaten track

- travelling across continents by train/bicycle/car/motor-bike etc.

With a little imagination and a lot of experience, setting down your travelling tales on paper could lead to endless opportunities, not least of which is to provide a realistic, atmospheric and exciting background for a fictional novel.

FINDING FUNNY MOMENTS

A sense of humour is one of the most useful assets any writer can possess.

Seeing the funny side

If you are one of those fortunate beings who has the capacity to see the funny side of even the most difficult situations, your writing will benefit a thousandfold.

Having fun with your hobby

Michael Green is one author who has made a successful career out of the humorous aspect of his hobbies. His *Coarse* series is required reading for every weekend sailor, rugby player, golfer and amateur actor.

With an innate ability to home in on the way the average person will go through hell and high water in the name of their favourite leisure activity, Michael's books keep you laughing from the very first line, as the opening to *The Art of Coarse Sailing* demonstrates.

Every year I swear I won't spend my holiday sailing again. Considering I say this annually, it's surprising how much sailing I've managed to do. Each time I return bruised, battered and suffering from incipient scurvy, with a great dent worn in my buttocks and I say, 'That was terrific fun but next year I'm going to do something restful'. And somehow twelve months later I'm banging the same dent in the same place with the edge of a cockpit coaming or crawling on hands and knees in some stinking bilge.

(*The Art of Coarse Sailing*, Michael Green, Arrow Books)

Michael has a gift for highlighting the romantic ideal and contrasting it with the less than pleasant reality. More importantly, he has a real enthusiasm for and knowledge of his subjects.

His *Coarse* books are not simply amusing accounts of his adventures, they are genuinely informative and packed with colourful characters who embellish and add to his misfortunes.

FOLLOWING WHERE YOUR IDEAS LEAD YOU

Writing non-fiction is a useful method of getting your ideas down on paper. It also helps you to understand the importance of accurate research and is a way of training you to work methodically and to a set routine.

Trying something new

Having identified just a few of the topics your past experience will equip you to write about, the next step is to sit down and do it.

CASE STUDIES
Val expresses her opinions

Val is a forceful lady in her mid-fifties. She writes clearly and expresses herself well on paper. She has written several articles complaining about a variety of goods and services which, although important to her, are neither topical nor of much interest to anyone else. She has tried to have her articles published in a number of women's magazines but to date, they have all been rejected.

Len takes life in his stride

Len lived and worked in Spain for several years up to his retirement, when he decided to return to the UK. He is easy-going with a ready wit and likes to try his hand at most forms of writing. He keeps a close eye on local issues and his witty, topical letters to the local newspaper are regularly printed. He is currently enjoying writing a series of humorous articles about his experiences living and working abroad.

CHECKLIST

1. Do you enjoy passing your expertise on to like-minded people?

2. Do you have something new and original to say?

3. Do you want to leave something for your family to remember you by?

4. Do you have an exciting story to tell?

5. Could you help both yourself and others by writing about your experiences?

ASSIGNMENT

Pick a topical item of local importance, preferably one which matters to you personally and write a letter about it to the editor of your local newspaper. Keep the letter brief and to the point and if you can, type it. Remember, for the best chance of publication, your letter should be just controversial enough to invite further comment.

3

Creating Fictional Characters

BASING CHARACTERS ON REAL PEOPLE

When interviewing authors plugging their latest book, one of the most frequent questions asked by the presenter is 'Are your characters based on real people?' The answer invariably given is 'Not exactly'.

In order to be convincing, fictional characters must ring true. The reader should be able to relate to them and identify with them, but the description needs only to be sufficient to project a recognisable image.

After all, as the average reader is unlikely to have met her, there is little point in faithfully producing an accurately detailed word-picture of Great-Aunt Edna. Worse still, if Edna had something of a reputation in her day, you could end up causing offence and even leaving yourself open to a possible lawsuit if you get your facts wrong.

Mixing and matching

The best way of avoiding this is to come up with a composite impression of Aunty which will satisfy interested relatives that she was the inspiration for your character, but is far enough removed to keep you out of the law courts.

As with an autobiographical account, mixing and matching enhances your characters and surprisingly, often helps to make them more believable.

Stereotyping and clichés

Stereotypes can be very useful in fiction. Used with caution, they offer an instantly recognisable framework on which to base your character.

However, writers who attempt to portray their own racist, sexist or socially stereotypical images invariably cause offence and these views do nothing to improve their characterisation.

We will be looking at political correctness in the chapter on children's writing but always bear in mind that without depth of personality, your characters will be clichéd and cardboard. It is essential, therefore, when building characters, that you know everything about them and can clearly visualise them in your own mind.

Giving them a past

Just like real people, fictional characters don't simply appear fully-grown. They have parents, backgrounds, siblings and experiences that shape their personalities and influence their current behaviour.

As soon as a suitable character comes into your head, be sure that you know what sort of person they are. Write a potted history or CV, as illustrated in the suggested format in Figure 3, which will give you an insight into their motivation for behaving as they do.

```
NAME: ...........................................................

AGE: ............................................................

APPEARANCE: ...............................................
(hair, eye colour, height, weight, build etc.)

MARITAL STATUS: ...........................................

CURRENT HOME: ............................................

OCCUPATION: .................................................

PARENTS: ......................................................
(alive or dead?)

SIBLINGS: ......................................................
(names, ages, marital status etc.)

CHILDHOOD: ..................................................
(happy, sad, traumatic etc.)

EDUCATION: ...................................................

QUALIFICATIONS: ............................................

RELATIONSHIPS: .............................................
(past and present)

PERSONALITY: ................................................

SPECIAL SKILLS: .............................................

STRENGTHS: ..................................................

WEAKNESSES: ................................................

ANY OTHER RELEVANT INFORMATION: ......................

........................................................................
```

Fig. 3. Suggested format for potted history.

Testing for realism

Whilst stereotyping can be a useful method of character-isation, be aware that different people have different perceptions. If you belong to a writers' circle or class, the following group exercise is a useful one:

1. Write a selection of job titles such as **teacher**, **plumber**, **TV presenter**, **sculptor**, **nurse** etc, on pieces of paper then distribute them among the group, allocating the same job title to two members at a time, e.g. if there are 8 group members, 2 will have teacher, 2 plumber and so on.

2. Ask each member to write their own description of the character the job title conjures up.

3. Now ask each member to read their description out in turn for the rest of the group to guess the job of the character being described.

Despite the fact that some of the group members will have been asked to write about the same character, the descriptions will probably be very different. Each image will, nevertheless, be an identifiable stereotype.

Seeing your characters in context

Having established that different people have different perceptions, another dimension to characterisation is the context in which your characters are set.

Using a TV Presenter from the above list as an example, there are a variety of options open to us, depending on the style, tone and genre of the novel. The character could be a:

- young, attractive ex-sportsman/woman, activity game-show host

- young anchor-man/woman for regional/national news programme

- investigative journalist for consumer programme

- ageing newsreader, concerned about fading looks

- ex-actor-turned-magazine-columnist, presenting afternoon magazine-style programme

- ex-pop-singer-turned-children's TV presenter

- ex-politician-turned-political interviewer/commentator.

The title 'TV Presenter' clearly has a very wide interpretation. The character can be male or female, young or ageing.

The one thing all of these characters have in common is that they work in a high-profile, fast-moving industry in which their status and job security is measured against their position in the viewing ratings.

Fitting into the storyline
Having determined the age, sex and personality of your character, he or she must now be placed into the context of the story you are writing.

VISUALISING BACKGROUNDS
Whether it is a thriller, romance, lifestyle or detective story, your character has to behave in a realistic and believable way. In order to do this, they must be seen to be the sort of person who would opt for the course of action you have in mind for them.

In her novel, *Hush-a-Bye*, author Susan Moody draws vivid word-pictures of her characters, all the while giving hints that their upbringing and backgrounds will have a profound influence on how they will react in the future.

In the following description of Harriet, the central character, there is a clear implication that parts of her childhood which she feels made little impact on her will prove to have been highly influential in her reaction to the situations in which she eventually finds herself:

> Harriet's mother had died when she was a baby. The fact of being an orphan had not, Harriet believed, affected her, apart from imbuing her with a spurious kind of glamour both in her own eyes and those of her school-friends. Most of these possessed the requisite number of parents; in other respects their lives and Harriet's were almost identical, their houses similar, the strictures placed upon them by adults the same. Growing up in a leafy, well-heeled London suburb, the loss of a parent by death was almost the only evidence any of them had seen of the misfortunes which could befall unluckier souls than themselves.

Harriet's father is a remote, undemonstrative figure and the influence of her relatively loveless early years is an integral part of the development of her character, particularly when, quite late in the book, her own baby is kidnapped.

Talking to each other

One of the most effective methods of characterisation is through the use of dialogue. How a character speaks will tell you an enormous amount about their attitude and personality.

We'll be looking at the techniques involved in writing realistic dialogue in a later chapter but for now, we need to think about our feelings towards the characters we create.

INVOLVING YOURSELF IN YOUR CHARACTERS' LIVES

We have seen how important it is to create backgrounds for our characters in order to give substance to them. We have also seen how their upbringing and backgrounds form the basis of the motivation for their actions.

Establishing motivation

Knowing the struggle your character may have had to achieve the status they have attained, you will instinctively know how they will react if they learn that everything they have worked for is to be taken away.

Returning to our TV Presenter, we can select a young anchor-woman for a regional news programme and devise both background and motivation for her. Using a chart format, Figure 4 details an unhappy childhood and difficulty sustaining relationships which suggests the following story-line for 26-year-old Sally Blake:

Motivation for young anchor-woman for regional news programme

A talent scout from a national news network has been following Sally's progress and offers her a job in their studio. She intends to take it when the offer is withdrawn. Mark, her influential lover, doesn't want to lose her on either a personal or professional level and has pulled strings to block the job offer.

NAME	Sally Blake
AGE	26
HAIR	Blonde, neatly-styled, shoulder-length
EYES	Blue, bright and smiling
BUILD	Slim, elegant
MOUTH	Sensitive, quite wide with fairly full lips showing white, even teeth
MARITAL STATUS	Single
CURRENT HOME	Functional flat near TV studio
PARENTS	Beth and James. Divorced when Sally was four. Father died recently, was a respected investigative reporter. Had little contact with his daughter. Mother – model, after divorce married fashion photographer, moved to France. Sent Sally to boarding school in UK when sister was born
SIBLINGS	Eighteen-year-old half-sister, Sophie, a model
STEPFATHER	Claude, has little interest in either Sally or Sophie. Absorbed in his work, he enjoys his glamorous jetsetting lifestyle. Has frequent affairs with young women
CHILDHOOD	Happy until divorce and Sophie's subsequent birth
EDUCATION	Hated boarding school and during holidays, fought with Sophie, who was educated at home in France
QUALIFICATIONS	Language Degree, 1st class honours from redbrick university
BOYFRIENDS	First real boyfriend was an activist in the student union, left her to move in with a drama student. Several short-term relationships since. Currently seeing Mark, a married chief executive in her TV company.
SPECIAL SKILLS	Speaks fluent French
STRENGTHS	Ambitious, level-headed in a crisis
WEAKNESSES	Scared of forming permanent relationships
RELEVANT INFORMATION	Sally is hardworking, conscientious and very ambitious. Scarred by her unhappy childhood and more recently, by the loss of her father, whom she emulates, she is determined to stop at nothing to reach the top of her profession

Fig. 4. First background for young, smart anchor-woman for regional news programme.

Based on what we already know about Sally's character, it is unlikely that she will give up without a fight or that there is any future in her relationship with Mark. She has never put family or friends before her own needs. She is a loner who was forced to take control of her own life from a very early age and is not going to be pushed around by someone who is trying to manipulate her for his own ends.

Her reaction
Armed with the information about Sally's background and character, depending on the style of the book, she could react in one of a number of ways. She could:

1. Blackmail Mark into using his influence to reinstate the job offer.

2. Devise a plan to murder Mark.

3. Confront Mark, fight with, and accidentally kill him.

4. Consult a lawyer and take Mark to court.

5. Compile an exposé of the TV industry.

6. Secretly conduct an in-depth investigation into corruption in Mark's company.

7. Set Mark up to take the blame for running a libellous news story.

Sally's reaction is determined by her tough background. The product of a less than perfect marriage, she has an absent father and a mother who transfers her affections to her new husband and baby with little thought to her daughter's feelings.

To her stepfather, she is an encumbrance, shipped off to boarding school to make way for her baby sister. It is not surprising that, as soon as she leaves university, Sally finds herself a flat in England and rarely returns to France.

She has been forced to become totally self-reliant and will take whatever action she deems necessary to achieve her aims.

CHANGING THE CHARACTER

However, if Sally's upbringing had been different, her reactions would change accordingly. Taking the same scenario, a few alterations here and there will produce a totally different result.

Rebuilding the background

Keeping the same framework, all we need to do is make a few adjustments to the attitudes of Sally's parents, change her schooling and her relationship with her sister and we have a whole new set of possibilities.

We'll still have the parents divorcing when she's four years old and her mother remarrying, but this time their attitude towards the child will be far more positive, as shown in the alterations to the chart in Figure 5.

Motivation

With this background, we now have a whole new set of reactions. When Sally's father dies, her family is supportive and caring. Her stepfather knows he cannot take her father's place but he is there if she needs him.

NAME	Sally Blake
AGE	26
HAIR	Blonde, neatly-styled, shoulder-length
EYES	Blue, bright and smiling
BUILD	Slim, elegant
MOUTH	Sensitive, quite wide with fairly full lips showing white, even teeth
MARITAL STATUS	Single
CURRENT HOME	Functional flat near TV studio
PARENTS	Beth and James. Divorced when Sally was four. Father died recently, was a respected investigative reporter. Saw Sally whenever he was on leave. Mother – model, after divorce married fashion photographer, moved to France. Sent Sally to boarding school in UK when sister was born
SIBLINGS	Eighteen-year-old half-sister, Sophie, a model. Irresponsible and fun-loving
STEPFATHER	Claude, good family man. Fond of Sally but feels a little intimidated by her determination to succeed and is aware that she idolised her father
CHILDHOOD	Happy. Very protective of Sophie, whom she looks out for when things go wrong, as they often do
EDUCATION	Loved boarding school in England but looked forward to holidays spent in France or in London with father whenever he was around
QUALIFICATIONS	Language Degree, 1st class honours from redbrick university
BOYFRIENDS	Has been refusing Mark, a married chief executive in her own TV company, for some time. Is admired from afar by Nick, a cameraman
SPECIAL SKILLS	Speaks fluent French
STRENGTHS	Ambitious but puts friends and family before career
WEAKNESSES	A little too trusting in her relationships
RELEVANT INFORMATION	Sally is hardworking, conscientious and ambitious. Although she loves her French family, she decided to live and work in the UK to be near her father. When he dies, she is left feeling vulnerable and frightened of the powerful Mark

Fig. 5. Second background for young, smart anchor-woman for regional news programme.

Storyline

With a supportive family and a happier disposition, Sally will be less aggressive, so we need to add an extra dimension to the storyline to trigger a reaction. We can utilise her half-sister Sophie who, whilst staying with Sally, falls in with a bad crowd, in which the powerful Mark plays a leading role.

Her reaction

Whilst she would no longer consider violence, points 4 to 6 above would almost certainly fit into the new scenario. Sally might:

♦ Consult a lawyer and take Mark to court.

♦ Compile an exposé of the TV industry.

♦ Secretly conduct an in-depth investigation into corruption in Mark's company.

The 'new' Sally wouldn't go it alone, she would seek help from a variety of sources:

1. The lawyer, with whom she becomes romantically involved.

2. The lovelorn cameraman, who risks his livelihood to help with her investigations.

3. Her stepfather, whose contacts in the media help her to rescue Sophie and put Mark behind bars.

4. Her father's papers – he was investigating Mark's activities just before he died.

5. Her mother, for support as a friend and confidante.

RELATING TO YOUR CHARACTER

Whichever scenario you choose, bear in mind that if you don't care about your character, neither will anyone else.

The 'old' Sally (Figure 4) may be ruthless but it's not her fault. As her creator, it is your task to convey her innermost thoughts and feelings to the reader so that they will understand the reasons behind her behaviour.

In order to truly relate to Sally, you need to put yourself in her place and imagine how you would feel if:

♦ When you were four years old, you saw your father leave home, never to return.

♦ After your father left, you felt utterly alone and abandoned.

♦ You were brought up by a selfish, spiteful mother.

♦ Without warning, your mother married a womaniser whom you hardly knew and who clearly disliked you.

♦ You were taken away to live in a foreign country.

♦ You were confronted with a baby sister then immediately packed off to boarding school.

♦ Your father died suddenly, severing the only link with memories of a happier time.

You would have to be particularly hard-hearted not to relate to at least one of the above circumstances. Adding this kind of depth to a character brings realism and is a major factor in obtaining that vital ingredient, reader identification.

Caring what happens

In our second characterisation of Sally (Figure 5), her background gives us little cause for concern. Despite her parents' divorce, she had a happy childhood so we need to rely on Sally's charismatic personality to gain the desired effect.

Once again, you have to put yourself in her place. You have everything going for you, happy family, comfortable home and excellent job prospects. Imagine how you would feel if, within an incredibly short timespan:

◆ Your father, whom you adored and emulated, died unexpectedly.

◆ A situation with which you were coping (i.e. Mark's unwanted advances) suddenly spiralled out of your control.

◆ You discovered that your beloved younger sister was in moral or physical danger.

◆ You felt you were falling in love at a time when everything in your life was being turned upside down.

In our second scenario, everything seems to be happening to Sally at once and as the author, you should be right in there with her, concerned for her, urging her to make the right decisions which, initially, she is unlikely to do, as we'll shortly discover in the following section dealing with conflict.

HOW WOULD YOU REACT IF THEY APPROACHED YOU?

Without realistic characters, a fictional story is flat and lifeless. People read about people, so the characters you create should not only be realistic, they should also provoke a reaction from your reader.

Running away

Every character in a work of fiction should be there for a purpose. Characters should never be used in order to set the scene or create a backcloth.

If you've placed them in a scene, they have to perform a function and with this in mind, you should either be attracted or repelled by them. If they only have a small role to play, you may simply find them interesting or intriguing but you should never be indifferent.

When creating fictional characters, therefore, imagine how you personally would react if you met them on a dark night. Would you:

◆ Run away?
◆ Stop to offer assistance?
◆ Fall in love?
◆ Be rooted to the spot in terror?
◆ Be filled with loathing?
◆ Attack them?
◆ Avoid making eye contact?
◆ Nod a brief greeting and move swiftly on?

One method of conveying exactly what sort of reaction your character would provoke is through interaction with another character.

Interacting with one another

In the following extract from the psychological thriller

Ladykiller by Martina Cole, a description of serial killer George Markham is given through the eyes of Josephine Denham, a colleague at work:

'Mr Markham, have you five minutes to spare?'

The voice of Josephine Denham broke into his thoughts. He turned in his seat to see her standing in the doorway, smiling at him.

'Of course, Mrs Denham.' His voice was soft and polite.

Josephine Denham turned and walked back to her office. George Markham gave her the creeps and she did not know why. He was always polite. Chillingly polite. He never took days off for no reason, he always kept himself to himself, never took long lunches or tried to engage her in banter, like some of the other male employees. All in all he was a model worker. Yet she had to admit to herself there was something about his soft, pudgy body and watery grey eyes that gave her the willies. She sat at her desk and observed the little man in front of her.

'Please, take a seat.'

She watched George take the material of his trousers between his thumb and forefinger and pull it up before sitting down. Even this action irritated her. She saw his funny little smile that showed his teeth and felt even more annoyed.

Provoking a reaction

The author leaves us in no doubt that George is most unsavoury and at no time do we feel the slightest bit of sympathy for him. Josephine has, we are sure, every right to dislike him. This impression is reinforced a few lines further on when we see his reaction as Josephine tells him he is to be made redundant.

> George felt an urge to leap from his chair and slap the supercilious bitch with her painted face, her dyed blonde hair, her fat, wobbling breasts. The dirty stinking slut! The dirty whore!

Whilst there is no doubt that George's vitriolic reaction is appalling, there is still room for a hint of justification. Anyone who has experienced redundancy must be able to relate to the feelings of frustration and helplessness welling up inside him.

At the same time, Josphine's unease in his presence is very well-founded as it is all too clear that any woman unfortunate enough to find herself alone with George Markham is in very grave danger.

CREATING CONFLICT

In order to understand the importance of conflict in a fictional tale, imagine the following scenario:

> A beautiful, titled young lady is about to celebrate her eighteenth birthday. Her wealthy, happily married parents throw a party for her at their stately home. Her adored older brother telephones to let her know that he is bringing his best friend and partner in his successful law firm to the party. The best friend is the handsome heir to a fortune and a vast estate in the country. Their eyes meet, they fall instantly in love to the great delight of their families. They marry, have

two children, a girl and a boy and live happily ever after.

By now, you are either shrugging and muttering 'So what?' or you're drifting off to sleep. Either way, it is unlikely that you found the above storyline exactly riveting because the simple fact of the matter is that nothing has gone wrong.

Throwing obstacles in the path

Conflict is all about obstructing the course of:

- true love
- solving a mystery
- obtaining revenge
- tracking someone down
- reaching a goal.

It is a sad fact of human nature that no one wants to read about anything that is easily gained. Your task as an author is to throw as many obstacles as possible in the path of your characters to ensure that we have to keep on reading if we are to discover whether they manage to achieve their aims.

CASE STUDIES

June makes everything all right

June is a cheerful person in her mid-twenties. The mother of two small children, she has an optimistic outlook on life and this is reflected in her characterisation. Unfortunately, this tendency always to look on the bright side means that her characters often lack depth and realism. She also finds it difficult to bring conflict into her stories, as she likes to make their lives run as smoothly as possible. Until she can overcome her desire to have everyone living happily ever after, her stories will continue to be dull and lifeless.

Bill takes a practical approach

Bill is a businessman in his late forties who travels extensively as part of his job both in the UK and abroad. The father of teenage children, he has had quite a chequered career, serving in the armed forces for a time and then as a prison officer. His past and present occupations have meant that he has learned how to relate to a wide variety of people on vastly different levels from all sectors of society. Consequently, he has developed the ability to predict how people are likely to react in stressful situations. He is currently writing a novel set against a background of the prison service which contains sufficient conflict and realism to make it compelling reading.

CHECKLIST

1. Do you really know your characters?

2. Have you created realistic backgrounds for them?

3. Do you know how they would react in a given situation?

4. How would you react if you met them?

5. Do you care what happens to them?

ASSIGNMENT

To help you understand how to build a character from a stereotype, try this rapid response exercise. Picture in your mind's eye a wealthy businessman, then answer the questions below using the first answer that comes into your head:

1. How old is he?

2. What colour are his hair and eyes?

3. How tall and what sort of build is he?

4. Is he nice or nasty?

5. What is his office like?

6. Where is it situated?

7. Is he married?

8. If yes, does he have a mistress?

9. What is his home like and where is it situated?

10. Does he have any children?

11. If yes, how many, what sex and how old are they?

12. Where is he now, at this moment?

13. What is he doing?

14. What will he do next?

NB: By now, you should be forming a storyline around his character.

④

Setting and Atmosphere

GETTING A FEEL OF PLACE AND TIME

Whenever and wherever your story is set, a thorough knowledge of the period and location about which you are writing is vital.

Using all five senses

You need to use all the five senses, **sight**, **sound**, **smell**, **touch** and **taste**, if you are to convey a feeling of time and place.

In the following extract from Susan Moody's novel *Husha-Bye*, her central character, Harriet, is staying with her grandparents. Opening with the sense of smell and continuing this as an overriding theme throughout the passage, the author skilfully brings all Harriet's senses into play to paint a vivid picture of the house and its occupants.

The house in Cornwall smelled different from the one in London: shinier, cleaner. Harriet's grandmother spent her time arranging flowers picked from her garden, polishing the furniture, filling the days with small routines, doing what she had done yesterday and what she would do again tomorrow. The lavender-scented sheets on their beds were starched and made of linen; there were starched napkins at meals too, with monograms in one corner. She did things in due season; made marmalade, collected windfalls, stirred Christmas puddings, cut the stalks of lavender and sewed the scented grains into sachets of lace and ribbon. Things were done at prescribed times; milk drunk at eleven, a walk at three, the radio switched on at 5.54 for the weather forecast before the six o'clock news.

Moving back and forth in time

The above passage does more than set the atmosphere, it also conveys an impression of time.

Harriet's grandmother is not a modern career woman. She is the epitome of respectability, comfortable with her role as wife and homemaker. She lives an ordered life in the country and her outlook is rooted in a strong sense of duty and the values of a previous generation.

Remove her from this setting and place her in a chrome and glass apartment in the centre of a bustling city and she will appear old-fashioned and vulnerable. Pulled out of her own time, she will be like a fish out of water and the atmosphere will become completely different.

Setting over characters

The importance an author gives to a story's setting depends not only on the style of writing but also on the genre. In a romance, for example, the background has a major influence on the behaviour of the characters. Listed below are just a few examples of settings taken from romantic novels:

* a Caribbean cruise ship
* a tropical island
* an Italian vineyard
* a lake in the Canadian Rockies
* an antiques shop and cottage in the country.

In each case, the setting is described in sensuous detail, the scents of fruits and flowers, crystal clear lakes, whispering breezes and rolling hills.

The pace of the story is always slow enough to allow the reader to savour the sights, sounds and flavours but fast enough to maintain the impetus.

Making war not love

Action novels such as war stories use similar techniques to conjure up the feel of battle. Shattered bodies and flattened buildings, deafening shellfire, screams of terror, the stench of death all around. Once bustling towns are reduced to piles of rubble and twisted metal, the surrounding landscape becomes a mass of craters littered with burned-out vehicles.

This time, the pace is very fast, pulling the reader through the horrific sights, sounds and smells as quickly as possible to the comparative safety of the next chapter.

Keeping the background out of the foreground

As a general rule, the setting should never be allowed to dominate the storyline. It is relatively easy to get carried away but try to avoid using more than ten lines of pure description in one block or your story will lose pace and fail to hold a reader's attention.

Letting your characters set the scene

The most effective way to describe a scene is to let your characters do it for you through interaction with their surroundings. This will improve the pace of your writing and convey a feeling of setting, atmosphere and insight into the character in one fell swoop.

For example, study the following two passages and decide which you feel is most atmospheric:

Passage A

It was the middle of winter. The room was icy cold and hiding in one corner was a child, a little girl. The man stood in the room for a moment but could not see her concealed in the dark shadows. He turned and strode away.

Passage B

No warmth from the thin winter sun had managed to penetrate the icy coldness of the room. The child huddled, shivering in one corner, willing the shadowy dimness to conceal her. She held her breath as the man stood motionless, listening for what seemed an eternity, before he turned and strode impatiently away.

VISITING LOCATIONS

There are pitfalls in setting your stories in real locations, particularly if you choose an area you moved away from and have not visited for many years.

To illustrate this, the following is just a small sample of recent changes in my own neighbourhood.

- The local high street has been decimated by the opening of an out-of-town shopping complex.

- A multiplex cinema is being constructed on the site of the former technical college.

- A series of mini-roundabouts have been built.

- Several roads have changed their use from two-way to one-way streets.

- A complex system of zebra crossings and pedestrian refuges has been constructed.

Changing the landscape

All over the country, roads are being widened, housing, trading and industrial estates are being built, supermarkets are springing up, golf courses and theme parks are changing the appearance of the landscape.

Conversely, many town and city centres have acquired a neglected, derelict look as unsuccessful businesses close and once-thriving factories stand empty, the surrounding areas overgrown with weeds and littered with glass from smashed windows.

Soaking up the atmosphere

It's not all gloom and doom of course. Much of the countryside has remained unchanged for generations and large tracts of land on old industrial sites have been reclaimed and landscaped by environmentalists.

If you intend to set your story in your own locality, you'll be up-to-date with any changes and have few problems

Soaking up the atmosphere

establishing a realistic atmosphere. If, however, you wish to set your story in the area where you grew up or lived some years ago, it is well worth revisiting the location in order to establish whether it still retains the atmosphere you wish to convey.

Striking a balance

Another problem with using a well-known location is that of striking the balance between instant recognition and distracting realism. The following passage details the progress of a character through the City of London.

> Leaving the Bank of England, Barnaby made his way to St Paul's Cathedral. He followed the route from Threadneedle Street to Cheapside, passing St Mildred's and Grocer's Hall Courts, Old Jewry, Ironmonger Lane and King Street on his right and Bucklersbury, Queen Street, Bow Lane and Bread Street on his left.

Whilst the famous names mentioned provide an unmistakable London setting, there is very little atmosphere in this

passage. There is the added difficulty, too, that anyone familiar with the area may well begin to wonder if the route and
road names are correct. At best, this will distract them from
the storyline and at worst, they may put the story down while
they go off and search for their *London A to Z*.

Drawing maps

As with any other writing technique, in the hands of a skilled
author, the use of this kind of detailed information can
become integral to the tone and pace of the book and
many writers can and do use it to great effect.

The attention to detail award-winning novelist Ruth Rendell pays to the routes taken by her protagonists, emphasises
rather than detracts from the atmosphere of her novels. She
sometimes takes this one stage further by drawing a map or
street plan of a location, as illustrated in Figure 6. Taken
from an Inspector Wexford novel entitled *Some Lie and
Some Die* (Arrow Books), the map depicts the location
for a pop festival in an area just outside the fictional
town of Kingsmarkham and not only helps the reader
get their bearings but also adds realism to the story.

Creating the feel of a place

For some novels, the setting is integral to the plot. Until its
demolition, the area surrounding the Berlin Wall was a central feature in scores of spy novels and the same is true of
famous landmarks such as the:

♦ Eiffel Tower
♦ Empire State Building
♦ Houses of Parliament

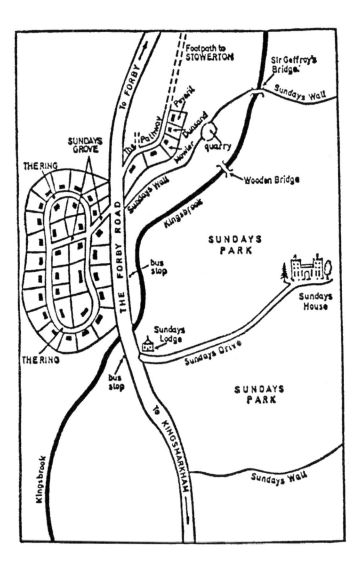

Fig. 6. Map of fictional location from Ruth Rendell's Inspector Wexford novel *Some Lie and Some Die* (Arrow Books), depicting the location for a pop festival in an area just outside the fictional town of Kingsmarkham.

- ◆ Kremlin
- ◆ St Mark's Square
- ◆ Statue of Liberty
- ◆ Taj Mahal.

Basing your setting on a familiar location

In order to avoid the distracting 'street map' scenario, an effective alternative is to throw in one or two well-known evocative names. This encourages the reader to use their imagination to fill in the blanks, as demonstrated by the following rewrite of the previous City of London example:

> Leaving the Bank of England, Barnaby made his way from Threadneedle Street towards St Pauls, feeling a flicker of excitement as he read off the historic names of the roads he passed. Old Jewry, Bow Lane, Bread Street, Cheapside. Barnaby recited them to himself as he tried, in vain, to block out the intrusive din of the modern-day traffic.

Making up your own location

Making up your own location allows you to design the landscape to suit your own purposes, particularly if it is based on an area with which you are very familiar.

It also allows you to deal with any unforeseen hazards constructed in your absence by the town planning department. The odd new road layout, housing or industrial estate can be happily discarded if it obstructs your protagonist's progress or detracts from the planned storyline and if you need to get from A to B in a hurry, you can simply build yourself an imaginary road.

Travelling to exotic places

As we have seen, romantic novels are by no means the only books which use foreign and exotic settings. Political thrillers, adventure novels, crime stories can all be set against exotic backgrounds and where science fiction and fantasy are concerned, the universe is your oyster.

However, reliance on a combination of travel guides, tourist brochures and memories of a seven-day package holiday to Benidorm is, on its own, unlikely to provide you with sufficient detail to create a realistically atmospheric background. If you are setting your story in a foreign country, your writing will be far more effective if you are thoroughly familiar with the area, its climate, people and politics.

This is fine if your story has a contemporary, earthbound setting but for historical or futuristic tales, research and educated guesswork are vital ingredients in the creation of the required atmosphere.

IMAGINING WHAT IT WOULD BE LIKE TO BE THERE

Assuming that you've done your research and have sufficient information to write a detailed description of your character's surroundings, try the following test:

> **Picture yourself sitting in an armchair in your living room. It is around 7.30 pm in the middle of winter and you are reading a book. You have a drink beside you. Now imagine exactly the same scene in a previous century and then at a point of your choosing in the future. For all three scenes, answer the questions listed below:**

1. What material has been used to make the chair you are sitting on?

2. What method of lighting are you using?

3. Is the room heated and if so how?

4. Is the room carpeted? If not, what sort of floor covering does it have?

5. How is the room decorated?

6. What is the title of the book you are reading?

7. What are you drinking?

8. Is it in a glass, cup, goblet, other? If not glass or china, what is it made of?

9. What are you wearing?

10. Are you warm enough?

By comparing how comfortable you normally feel in the given situation with how you imagine it would have felt in the past and how it might feel in the future, you can bring a great deal of realism to your writing.

Living the part

One advantage historical settings have over futuristic ones is that lifestyles, costume, homes, furnishing and utensils of previous generations are very well documented. Research material is available in the form of books, paintings, antiques, published letters, historic buildings, museums, newspapers and for more recent history, photographs and films.

Making an educated guess

For historical settings, we have sufficient information to imagine how our characters related to their surroundings. The only disadvantage is that, if you get it wrong, someone is bound to notice.

In contrast, stories set in the future offer more leeway to let the author's imagination run riot but the designs, materials and lifestyles depicted must be based on current scientific knowledge.

WEARING DIFFERENT CLOTHES AND COSTUMES

The costumes your characters wear do much more than just set the scene. Among other things, they:

◆ set the period
◆ set the age, nationality and occupation of a character
◆ give an insight into the character's personality
◆ convey a sense of occasion
◆ evoke reader identification.

To help you relate to the way a character would move and respond in various situations, imagine how you react when you are wearing clothes designed for a specific purpose. If you have ever worn one or more of the following outfits, for example, how did you feel and how did you move around the room?

◆ a full-length evening dress
◆ top hat and tails
◆ a wedding dress and veil
◆ a dinner jacket and dress shirt

- a business suit
- old jeans and tee shirt
- overalls
- luxurious silk underwear
- thermal underwear
- wellington boots
- nothing at all.

Acting the part

Take top hat and tails from the above list. They have a seemingly magical effect on their wearer so that men not exactly renowned for their sartorial elegance suddenly find themselves holding their shoulders back and their stomachs in. Perched at a jaunty angle on their heads, the top hat provides the perfect finishing touch, conveying both style and breeding.

The same is true of the full-length ball gown. Ladies who usually dress for comfort in tee shirts and jeans can find themselves transformed into Cinderella look-alikes at the drop of a neckline. Exchange the squashy trainer for the satin slipper and you have a picture of elegance and femininity in not only her looks but also her demeanour and actions.

Conforming or contrasting

The fact that the clothes your hero is wearing have him looking every inch the gentleman and your heroine's attire implies style and breeding is a major factor in characterisation.

Whilst the tall, handsome, immaculately turned-out chap may fulfil the role of every woman's answer to her dreams, he could also be any one of the following:

- a confidence trickster without a penny to his name

- a fashion-conscious young dandy, interested only in his own appearance

- a charming rogue, who overspends on clothes, wining, dining and gambling

- a man of action, uncomfortably restricted by his formal clothes.

The way he wears his clothes, his bearing, attitude and behaviour will all give a clue to his personality. Does he, for example, constantly rub his finger round his shirt collar, indicating discomfort? Or is he unable to pass a mirror without stopping to check the condition of his silk pocket handkerchief?

Heroines, too, reveal a great deal from the way they cope with their clothes. Dressed in skin-tight evening gown and dripping with diamonds, our heroine could be:

- a confidence tricker without a penny to her name

- a vain gold-digger, determined to trap a rich husband

- a shy, sporty-type restricted and uncomfortable in these clothes.

Like her male counterpart, our heroine may be sophisticated and elegant but if she has difficulty walking in her tight skirt or modesty has her constantly pulling up the top of her dress, it will be clear that she is less than comfortable with the image she is expected to project.

CASE STUDIES

Ivy looks back

Ivy was brought up in a rural village but has lived most of her adult life in the city. Prompted by nostalgia, she decides to set her contemporary novel in the area where she spent her childhood and describes the surrounding countryside in meticulous detail. Fortunately, she decides to visit her old home before she completes the novel, to discover an out of town shopping complex now covers the farmland where most of the present day action of her story takes place.

Rachel demolishes an office block

Rachel has the perfect location in mind for the fictional city setting of her historical novel. There is now an office block on the site but, with the aid of some careful research, she unearths sufficient information about the houses which once stood there to create a vividly realistic impression of the layout of city streets at the time in which her story is set. Based on her investigations, she is able to devise her own street map for reference, adapting it to suit the storyline wherever necessary.

CHECKLIST

1. Are you thoroughly familiar with the location you are using?

2. Do you have a map of the area?

3. Have you calculated distances and travel times?

4. Do you know what mode of transport your characters would use?

5. Are you confident you know how it feels to live in your chosen period?

6. Are the costumes accurate and do you know how it feels to wear them?

ASSIGNMENT

Select one of the following castles and describe it as seen through the eyes of a visitor:

- a Disney-style theme park fantasy
- a stately home, open to the public
- a highland fortress
- a ruin
- an urban castle
- a bouncy castle.

(**NB**: This exercise works well in pairs within a group. The description is given by one pair and the others have to guess what sort of castle is being described.)

5

Showing Not Telling

REACTING AND INTERACTING WITH PEOPLE AND SURROUNDINGS

As we saw in the previous chapter, one of the most effective ways to convey personality, age, setting and atmosphere is through the reactions of your characters.

This involves *showing* what is happening through a combination of action, reaction and dialogue rather than narrating or *telling* the story to the reader.

Telling

Writers tend to be avid readers, often with a background steeped in classic works of literature, many of which are written in the narrative voice. One example of this technique is Emily Brontë's classic novel *Wuthering Heights*, where the sequence of events is related in story form by one minor character to another.

It is perfectly understandable that well-read writers should seek to emulate this approach but in a modern context, the technique is very dated. It slows the pace considerably and by the time the scene is set, both you and the reader may well have forgotten what the story was about in the first place.

Moving with the times

It is a testament to the skill of our classic authors that their

Moving with the times

stories continue to be enjoyed today. One reason for this is that, despite the 'Let me tell you a story...' quality of the writing, many classic tales contain far more action and inter-action than you may think. It is the narrative style that creates the misleading impression of a leisurely pace, not the actual content of the story.

Showing

In contrast to using a static character to 'tell' the tale, *showing* what is happening through the actions and reactions of your characters brings pace, movement and life to a story, as you can see by comparing the following examples:

Example A (telling)

The weather was very cold. Luckily, Susan had put on her heavy overcoat, the one with the hood, so she was able to keep reasonably warm. Walking along the road, she no-ticed that there were no leaves on the trees, a sure sign of winter. The windows of the houses on either side of the pavement were blank and dark. Susan thought it made the street feel gloomy and oppressive.

Example B (showing)
Susan pulled her heavy overcoat around her to keep out the icy cold. Offering silent thanks for the warm, fur-lined hood, she hurried down the deserted street. Leafless trees waved menacingly in the bitter wind as she anxiously surveyed the blank windows of the houses lining the bare pavements. The oppressive gloom of her surroundings sent a shudder of fear through Susan's slender frame.

Doing and describing

By comparing the two passages above you can see that in Example A, Susan is almost static. The reader is told that the weather is cold, that Susan is wearing a heavy, hooded overcoat, that the street was gloomy and the atmosphere oppressive.

In Example B, however, Susan is reacting to her surroundings. She 'pulls' her heavy overcoat around her, 'offers silent thanks' for its warmth and 'hurries' down the street. The trees, too, are moving. They are 'waving menacingly' causing her to become anxious. There is more description too, as the 'oppressive gloom' sends a 'shudder of fear' through her.

Performing actions

Through the use of verbs and adverbs, your characters will perform actions that demonstrate clearly their reaction to the situation in which they find themselves.

This is a far more economical method of writing description than the narrative style. In fact, Example A is 70 words long, whilst example B, with all the extra information about Susan's build, her coat and her frame of mind etc., amounts to only 64.

FEELING THE HEAT

Having established that our characters must react to the conditions around them, we have to think about how they will behave in a variety of circumstances.

Hotting up

In the following passage from Jonathan Gash's novel, *The Judas Pair* (Arrow Books), antiques dealer and amateur sleuth Lovejoy finds himself in mortal danger, when the villain sets fire to the thatched roof of his cottage.

> Then I smelled smoke.
> The shushing sound was the pooled noise of a million crackles. My thatched roof had been fired, probably by means of a lighted arrow.

At this point, Lovejoy panics but his sense of self-preservation swings into action and he makes a rapid analysis of his situation:

> I had to think. Smoke was beginning to drift in ominous columns vertically downwards. Reflected firelight from each window showed me more of the living-room than I'd seen for some time. I was going to choke to death before finally the flames got me. The beams would set alight, the walls would catch fire and the fire would extend downwards until the entire cottage was ablaze.

Lovejoy realises that his only hope is to bury himself in a priest's hole under the flagstone floor but he is unprepared for the conditions he encounters:

The air entering my lungs was already searingly hot. From above my head came frantic gushing sounds, creakings and occasional ponderous crashes which terrified me more than anything. The walls would be burning now and the beams would be tumbling through the living-room ceiling. Twice I heard loud reports as the glass windows went. It must be an inferno. I was worn out and dying from heat. Too clever by far, I'd got myself in the reverse of the usual position. I was safe from smoke and being cooked in an oven. If only I could bring air in.

I forced myself to think as the blaze above my head reached a crescendo. What could make air move?

All through the passage, Lovejoy is reacting to his surroundings and the rising temperature. He is faced with a race against time and in order to convey this, the author flicks back and forth between the raging inferno above Lovejoy's head and the extreme heat of his confined conditions in the priest's hole under the floor. This keeps the pace moving extremely quickly, pulling the reader along so that they, too, can feel the heat, smell the smoke and sense the terror Lovejoy is experiencing.

SHIVERING AGAINST THE COLD

As we have already seen in some of the examples used, our characters' reactions to temperature will be reflected in their behaviour.

Cooling down

There are a variety of ways to convey the impression that a character is feeling the cold. They may:

- shiver
- pull their coat more tightly around them
- carefully select warm clothing to wear
- flap their arms
- stamp their feet
- huddle together for warmth
- feel sleepy, risking death if they close their eyes
- keep moving to increase their circulation.

Weathering the storm

Whether hot, cold, wet or dry, one thing you have to remember is not to overdo climatic conditions. The following passage illustrates this point:

> It had been raining hard for days. Water streamed from the gutters of every roof, pouring down windows, along pavements, running in fast moving rivulets along each road. Underneath the streets, torrents of water gushed and gurgled beneath the feet of the people hurrying along the shiny, wet pavements, pushing and shoving one another in their haste to get out of the rain. Steel grey storm clouds gathered overhead, meeting one another head on in preparation for yet another downpour. It was very, very wet. (85 words)

Feeding in the information

One method of avoiding this kind of over-emphasis is to feed the information to the reader in snippets.

If it is raining heavily, then have your character run for shelter, or struggle for a few seconds with an uncooperative umbrella. An impression conveyed with a few well-chosen verbs, adverbs and adjectives will be far more effective than wordy description, hammering home a point made early in the first sentence.

Economy with words not only improves the quality of your writing, it also makes your work a more attractive proposition for prospective publishers. Bearing this in mind, try rewriting the above passage in a more effective and subtle way. You will find that, by cutting out any superfluous information and including a character to react to the conditions, the piece will be far more evocative and probably a lot shorter.

(A suggested rewrite of the above exercise can be found at the back of the book.)

REVEALING EMOTIONS

We all have emotions which reveal themselves through our writing and there are certain circumstances to which we react more strongly than others.

Whilst our characters need not be based on ourselves or on our nearest and dearest, our own emotions will be reflected in their reactions and behaviour.

Standing up for yourself

You may, for example, have been bullied in the past by someone in a position of power, a teacher, employer, parent or spouse. As a result of this experience, bullying behaviour in anyone you encounter will evoke some very strong feelings. These can and should be harnessed and used to great effect by your characters.

If you feel strongly about something, so will your characters but unless you believe implicitly that they will react in a certain way, then your portrayal will be unrealistic.

EXPRESSING FEELINGS

Allow your characters to do the talking for you. Whilst it is important that your characters react as they, not you, would in a given situation, you'll be amazed at how often your attitudes and opinions are reflected in their actions.

Thinking positively

There is no reason why emotions should be negative. Positive attitudes work every bit as well as negative ones and enthusiasm always comes over in an author's work.

It may be a lifestyle, an ideal, a sport or a certain type of person but whatever your passion, you can convey it very effectively through the character you write about and add realistic backgrounds to your stories at the same time.

Writing as I do for the women's magazine market, my characters' attitudes and opinions reflect my own but must also relate to the readership of the magazine.

The extract below, from a short story entitled 'Wishing', illustrates the frustration an intelligent, hardworking businesswoman feels when trapped in a marriage with a dominant husband. She has found what she considers to be her dream home but her husband controls the finances and has to be persuaded that the property is a good investment before he will consider parting with her hard-earned cash.

Watching Martin pace round the outside of the building, Lisa could almost see the figures being calculated within his brain.

She sighed, wondering why his head for business had ever attracted her to him. A young accountant who knew a good thing when he saw it, Martin had seized the opportunity to show the inexperienced fashion student how to market the hand-made knitwear she was producing.

In the eighteen years since they'd married, the home-based operation had grown into a thriving, designer label company.

She squared her shoulders, determined to fight off the familiar knot of disappointment that Martin's attitude was causing in her stomach.

Throughout the story, Martin's reaction to everything Lisa shows him is cold and disinterested. Determined not to lose her dream, Lisa explores the grounds and is delighted to find a wishing well, complete with thatched roof, concealed in the neglected garden.

She intends to breed sheep on the land in order to produce wool for her garments and is even more pleased when the house agent assures her that the well is real and the water pure.

Unfortunately, Martin fails to see the potential of the property, either romantic or financial, and in a last ditch attempt to persuade him otherwise, Lisa lures him towards the wishing well. The story's ending was, for me, more than satisfactory in dealing with the injustice of Lisa's situation:

A sudden thought caused Lisa to frown. As she opened the car door and reached for the mobile phone, she wondered whether the well might be polluted. Admittedly Mr Peters had insisted that the water was pure but things were a little different now.

No. Lisa shook her head firmly. Nothing could go wrong. Especially as she'd made a wish. Which is what you always did, wasn't it? Just before you threw something into a wishing well.

(*Bella*, 1993)

It is not only the sense of a wrong righted that vindicates Lisa in the appalling crime she has committed but also her almost childlike innocence in chasing an elusive dream.

She and I had absolutely nothing in common in looks, age and, thankfully, our choice of husband but I couldn't help feeling sorry for her and wanting her to have her wish and it was this element that brought her character alive and made the story work for me.

MOVING YOUR CHARACTERS AROUND THE ROOM

As we saw in the section dealing with reaction and interaction, static characters are dull and lifeless. If you are to breathe any life into them, they must be seen to move about.

In order to write effectively about a situation, it is not enough just to visualise the characters, the author must also have a clear picture of their surroundings. The layout of a room, for example, the length of a road, the interior of a car.

Minding the furniture

Even when all the characters are seated, they still nod their heads, shift position, wave a hand expressively. They may stand up, pace the carpet or make their way into another room. In order to convey this effectively, you need to know the layout of not only the room but also the building and how they can get to where they want to go.

You also need to know where the furniture is placed, how they manoeuvre around it and how fast or slowly they move.

SPEEDING AND SLOWING THE PACE WITH VOCABULARY

Throughout any story, an author has to increase and slow the pace in order to gain the maximum effect. This is achieved by a combination of emotive vocabulary and the length of the words and sentences used.

Shortening and lengthening the sentence

As a general rule, short words and sentences denote:

- anger
- urgency
- fear
- pain.

Longer words and sentences denote:

- romance
- contentment
- relaxation
- confidence.

You can also use longer, slower sentences to help build tension as in the following extract from Martina Cole's suspense novel *The Ladykiller*:

> It was Saturday and George was alone in the house. After carefully washing up the breakfast things and putting them away, he made himself a pot of tea. While it brewed on the kitchen table he walked down to his shed and brought back his scrapbooks.

At first sight, this scene portrays a contented man relaxing in his home on a Saturday morning. By this stage in the book, however, the reader is painfully aware of the horrific images that George's 'scrapbooks' contain.

Now compare the lengths of both the words and the sentences in the above extract with the following passage from the same book:

> The two small boys walked fast. Driving rain was pelting into their faces. The smaller of the two had red-rimmed eyes and had obviously been crying. A large clap of thunder boomed overhead, followed by a flash of lightning that lit up the sky.
> (*The Ladykiller*, Martina Cole, Hodder Headline)

The pace of the second passage is much faster than the first. In both cases the reader is in no doubt that something very unpleasant is about to happen but in the first example, the character is content and this is reflected in the vocabulary used. In the second extract, the characters are clearly unhappy and the vocabulary is short, sharp and threatening.

FLASHING BACK AND FORTH IN TIME

Flashback is one of the most useful tools a writer can use. It:

- provides an insight into your characters' personalities and pasts

- gives background information

- describes the characters and adds substance to the plot

- moves the story forward

- offers hints or 'signposts' that history is about to repeat itself.

Flashing information

Whilst the length of a flashback varies considerably from one short phrase to a complete chapter, the technique works best if you simply 'flash' to a significant incident in the past, then bring your character straight back to the present as soon as you have imparted the relevant information.

For example, if the reader is to understand why our TV presenter, Sally Blake, behaves in a certain way, we need to give them a few hints about the background to the story. The flashbacks in the following scene are marked in italics:

'I'm sorry Mark,' Sally fought back the tears which threatened to overwhelm her resolve, 'It's over. I'm leaving you. *I shouldn't have believed your lies about leaving your wife and children.*'

Hugging her knees to her chin, she rocked childishly to and fro for comfort, waiting in vain for his response, 'Did you hear what I said?'

'Oh, yes, I heard you.'

Sally felt the hairs on the back of her neck stand on end as she unclasped her legs and lifted her head to meet his furious gaze. *The last time he'd used that tone, the violence that had followed had landed her in hospital.* Furtively, she slid sideways across the bed, increasing the distance between them.

Flashbacks should provide a series of revelations about the characters which give just enough information to keep the reader wanting to know more but at the same time, reveal something the reader didn't know before.

In the above example, the first flashback informs us that Mark is a married man, the second that he is violent. From these two snippets of information, we know the background to their relationship and can predict a negative reaction to Sally's desire to end it.

Key phrases

Listed below are some key phrases designed to lead you smoothly into flashback:

- That summer had been almost perfect.
- There had been a time when things were different.
- As a child, he had been nervous and shy.

Filling a whole chapter

Whilst it is possible to write whole chapters in flashback, this can be counter-productive. As always, in the hands of a skilled author, lengthy flashback of this type can be very effective.

However, for it to work well, the content must be completely riveting and integral to the main plot. Even then, it can sometimes be difficult to pull the reader back to the present. It is usually better to stick to brief, rapid flashes to keep your story moving smoothly and at a good pace.

Moving forward in time

It can be surprisingly difficult to move your characters forward from one place and time to the next.

For example, when getting them from work to home, unless it is vital to the plot, there is no point in having them walk out of the building, get into their car and giving a blow by blow account of the drive home.

Nor is there any need, once they are home, to follow their progress through eating their evening meal, going to bed, then getting up in the morning, leaving the house and driving back to work again.

How, therefore, do you get your characters from A to B and from one day to the next without slowing the pace?

Stopping and starting

The solution is relatively easy. You simply stop at the end of one piece of action and start up again at the next. For example:

> She picked up her handbag and walked briskly to the door, 'See you tomorrow then,' she nodded curtly in my direction, 'I'll see myself out.'
> She arrived promptly at nine the next morning.

Once again, there are key phrases that are helpful in moving the action forward.

◆ It wasn't until much later that . . .

◆ It was to be years, not days, before they would meet again.

◆ Less than an hour had passed before . . .

CASE STUDIES
Gary includes every detail
Gary is extremely keen to write action novels and once he starts to write, the words tumble onto the page. His story ideas are exciting and imaginative but his tendency to include large tracts of background information and longwinded description produce static characters, lacking realism. Sadly, the superfluous information in his stories makes them over-complicated and confusing to read.

Steve tries out his climbing skills
Steve's hobby is climbing and he bases his plot development on situations he has encountered as a member of a climbing team. By combining his experiences of climbing different types of terrain, in a variety of weather conditions with his knowledge of teamwork in potentially dangerous situations, he is able to bring his characters vividly to life. As a result, his adventure stories are fast-paced and exciting.

CHECKLIST
1. Do your characters react to their surroundings?

2. Do they interact with one another?

3. Have you clearly conveyed their surroundings?

4. Do you know how their past governs their present behaviour?

5. Do they fight for your principles?

6. Does the pace set the mood effectively?

7. Are your flashbacks short and effective?

8. Does each scene move smoothly into the next?

ASSIGNMENT

Write a scene in which a wife is trying to conceal a murder weapon immediately after killing her husband. The scene should contain the following information:

- the wife's appearance, including height, hair style, age and build
- the time of day
- the season
- the room she is in
- how the room is furnished
- why she killed him.

6

Writing Realistic Dialogue

DEVELOPING A GOOD EAR

Dialogue is the bearer of information, plot and character-isation. It performs a number of vital functions for the fiction writer:

- Delineates character.
- Moves the story forward.
- Creates conflict, tension and suspense.
- Explains what happened in the past.
- Conveys emotion.
- Conveys the thoughts of the characters.

Perhaps most importantly of all, dialogue between your characters brings them to life in a way that no other writing technique can.

Hearing them speak

Until a character speaks, all their thoughts and emotions are portrayed through someone else's eyes, i.e. the narrator's.

The things a character says and the way they say them gives a much clearer insight into their character and allows the reader to make up their own mind as to what sort of person they might be.

Realistic dialogue gives immediate characterisation in a way that narrative simply cannot do. As a quick test, read through the following phrases and see who you think is speaking:

1. 'For goodness' sake get your hair out of your eyes and stand up straight when I'm talking to you.'

2. 'I can spare you five minutes but keep it brief.'

3. 'Hold my hand while we cross the road.'

4. 'Good morning, how may I help you?'

Not only do we have an instant idea of the person speaking but we can also make an educated guess about their appearance and their expression.

For no. 1, for example, the image is immediately of someone in authority, a parent or teacher, and their expression is stern, their demeanour impatient.

By contrast, example no. 4 is probably smiling and is making an effort to be polite and friendly. He or she is almost certainly dressed smartly in order to make a good impression on a potential customer.

Sounding realistic

If you were to write a completely realistic piece of dialogue between two young women, it might sound something like this:

'Hi! How's it going?'
'OK. How's things with you?'
'Oh, you know, OK but I, er...'

'Yeah, I know but you can't, well, um, you know.'

'Yeah, I know but anyway, did you watch 'Soapsuds' last night? Wasn't it awful?'

'The pits. She'd never have done that in real life. I mean, erm, well, it's so...'

'Yeah, I know.'

Interrupting, 'umming' and 'aahing'

In real life, most people sprinkle their conversations with 'ums' and 'aahs'. They also tend to interrupt the person speaking to them, so that sentences are cut short in mid-flow.

If fiction writers were to include this sort of dialogue in their stories, no one would read past the first piece of conversation. In fiction, each character must have their say in their own instantly recognisable voice.

In order to produce realistic dialogue, therefore, you have to develop a good ear for listening to how the people around you speak and an ability to transfer their 'voices' onto the page in an acceptable way.

ACTING OUT A SITUATION

One method of developing realistic voices for your characters is to act out the situation you wish to portray.

Recording the speeches

You can do this by imagining it in your head or by speaking the words out loud to hear how they sound.

You may prefer to record all the dialogue on tape so you can play it back at your leisure and ensure that each character has their own distinctive way of speaking.

Use the method which works best for you but make sure that if one character says, 'Hello, how are you?', the response is 'I'm fine, how are you?' and not something entirely unrelated.

Communicating with each other

Remember that the purpose of writing dialogue is to get your characters communicating with each other, not talking directly to the reader.

The technique of having one character saying something, whilst the other talks either to themselves or to the audience about something completely different is best left to script-writers who have the advantage of the visual and aural dimensions to explain what is going on.

Having a conversation

One useful method of bringing your dialogue to life is to choose the pair you most strongly identify with from the list below and write a confrontational conversation between them:

* Dissatisfied customer/unhelpful shop assistant.
* Unreasonable traffic warden/irate motorist.
* Disinterested hospital receptionist/frantic patient.
* Officious train guard/exasperated commuter.
* Harassed shopper/pushy elderly lady.
* Angry homeowner/selfish neighbour.

If, by now, you are in a flaming temper, calm yourself down by reading what you have written. The dialogue should be wonderfully realistic and vibrant.

Putting the speech in context

The vocabulary your characters use conveys more than just personality, it also gives an idea of their age, social status and relationship to one another. Read the two examples below and see if you can tell who the characters might be:

Example A

'You're not going out tonight. I won't let you.'
'You can't stop me, I'm old enough to do as I like.'
'You're not so old that I can't give you a clip round the ear.'
'But I've got to go, everyone's going.'

Example B

'You're not going out tonight. I won't let you.'
'You can't stop me, I'll do as I like.'
'If you go I'll kill myself.'
'Don't be a fool.'

Altering the vocabulary

The characters speaking in Example A are most likely to be a parent and child, probably a teenager.

In Example B, we have an entirely different situation. Here the characters are clearly lovers, heading towards a break-up in their relationship.

In essence, it is the same conversation but the things the characters say, the vocabulary they use, the way they speak, are quite different.

He said, she said

Take a look at the following passages and decide which you think works best:

Passage A

'You know I hate fish,' he said, 'Yet every week without fail, you insist on trying to make me eat it,' he complained, throwing down his knife and fork in disgust.

Passage B

'You know I hate fish,' he threw his knife and fork down in disgust. 'Yet every week without fail, you insist on trying to make me eat it.'

In fact, both passages work perfectly well but in Passage A, the words 'he said' and 'he complained' are completely superfluous.

Combining action and dialogue

As we saw in the previous chapter, characters are not static. They move from place to place, wave their hands around, shrug their shoulders and stamp their feet.

Their facial expressions change, they have endearing or irritating mannerisms and their body language can tell you almost as much about them as the way they actually speak.

A combination of action and dialogue, as demonstrated in Passage B above, will bring far more realism and life to the characters than a string of 'he/she says'.

Standing alone

For short passages, good dialogue will stand alone without any action at all as you can see from the following conversation between a customer and a shop assistant:

> 'I bought this tape player yesterday and it doesn't work.'
> 'I see. What's the problem?'
> 'It keeps chewing up the tapes.'
> 'I see. What would you like us to do about it?'
> 'Give me a replacement of course.'
> 'I'll have to get clearance from the manager but he's at lunch right now.'
> 'OK. I'll wait.'

There is no problem understanding the situation. We can easily tell which one is speaking and the dialogue flows perfectly well.

Within the context of a story where we are familiar with the characters and the plot, a short conversation like this keeps the action moving very effectively. It should not, however, be sustained for too long for a number of reasons:

♦ Unless we know the characters beforehand, we have no idea what they look like.

♦ It is more difficult to assess the mood of the characters.

♦ No matter how distinctive the voices, the conversation will eventually become confusing.

♦ A long block of unbroken dialogue soon becomes boring.

Bringing in some action

Action serves as the descriptive element within dialogue as you can see from the following rewrite:

> 'I bought this tape player yesterday and it doesn't work,' Colin slapped the box down on the counter.

'I see. What's the problem?'

'It keeps chewing up the tapes,' irritably, he tipped the device out of its packing.

'I see,' smiling helpfully, the girl picked it up and began turning it around in her hands in a vain attempt to detect the fault. 'What would you like us to do about it?'

Colin sighed impatiently, 'Give me a replacement of course.'

The girl frowned, 'I'll have to get clearance from the manager,' she chewed nervously at her lip, 'but he's at lunch right now.'

'OK.' Colin snatched up the tape player and stuffed it back into its box, 'I'll wait.'

From their actions, we can see that the girl is anxious to please but has no idea how to deal with the situation. Colin, on the other hand, is irritable and not about to be palmed off by an inexperienced youngster.

LOSING YOUR TEMPER

In the middle of domestic arguments with their loved ones, it is not unknown for authors to stop dead in mid-insult and reach for their trusty notepad and pen.

Fighting talk

A keen writer will never let a good piece of dialogue escape, no matter when or where they stumble across it. If their partner happens to hurl a particularly juicy phrase at them in the heat of battle, they know they'll only regret it if they don't stop and write it down.

We all find ourselves in confrontational situations from time to time and the more you can identify with the roles of your characters and relate to their feelings and frustrations the more realistic their arguments will sound.

Basing your characters' dialogue on your own domestic disputes may seem heartless and insensitive but for the true creative writer, there's no sense in wasting good material.

FALLING IN LOVE

Conflict is a vital element in any work of fiction, so the dialogue between two characters falling in love should be as volatile as arguments between warring partners.

Whispering sweet nothings

Whilst tender pillow-talk has its place, all the concerns, heartache, soul-searching and nerves that are part and parcel of forming a new relationship must be reflected in the dialogue.

If every conversation is dripping with sugary sweet declarations of love, it will not only sound unrealistic but also be utterly boring. In order to convey heightened sexual attraction between two characters, there must be an element of tension in the dialogue.

In novelist Patricia Burns' First World War saga, *Cinnamon Alley*, heroine Poppy Powers meets and falls for American serviceman, Scott Warrender. To complicate matters, she is already being ardently pursued by veteran Joe Chaplin.

The following short extract leaves the reader in no doubt about her feelings towards the two men:

Then Scott gave her a brief hug and let her go.

'I guess I better let you get back to work. But I'll be watching you, mind. I'll be watching every move you make.'

When Joe said things like that it irritated her. From Scott, it made her feel cared for and secure.

(*Cinnamon Alley*, Patricia Burns, Arrow Books)

CREATING REALISTIC ACCENTS AND DIALECTS

So far, all the conversations we have looked at have been in standard English but this isn't always the case.

If your story has a regional or foreign influence, part of the characterisation may hinge on the protagonist having an instantly recognisable accent and this has to be conveyed to the reader.

Avoiding the apostrophe

Let's take a well-known quotation by Robert Burns:

Wee, sleekit, cow'rin tim'rous beastie,
O' what a panic's in thy breastie.

(To a Mouse)

To anyone familiar with the quote, deciphering it on the printed page is relatively easy but for many, a long tract of unfamiliar words littered with apostrophes is a highly unattractive, not to say unreadable, proposition.

Listening to the rhythm

Rather than try to reproduce an accent phonetically by spelling the words differently or dropping the odd letter here and there and replacing it with an apostrophe, listen to the rhythm of speech.

You can achieve far more realism by turning the order of words around in a sentence and sparingly throwing in the odd colloquialism.

In contrast to her Scottish namesake, contemporary novelist Patricia Burns effectively conveys Scott Warrender's American accent through the subtle use of phraseology and in Poppy's reaction to the things he says, as shown in the following extract:

> Poppy tucked her hand inside his elbow.
> 'You'll have to tell me which way to go. Is it far? I hope so.'
> 'I usually get the first workmen's tram,' Poppy told him, before she could stop herself.
> 'To hell with that – begging your pardon – we'll find a cab. Are you tired?'
> Generally she was worn out at the end of a night spent on her feet, wanting only to crawl into bed and sleep the sleep of the dead. But tonight she could have run all the way to Scotland and back.
> 'No, not a bit. I'm fine.'
> 'You're tougher than me, then. When I was waiting tables I was washed out by the time I finished.'
> 'You? A waiter? But you're an officer.'
> 'Don't mean a thing, honey. My folks keep a hardware store in upstate Pennsylvania. I worked my way through college.'
> 'Oh' – It was like a foreign language, but she did get the gist of it.
>
> (*Cinnamon Alley*, Patricia Burns, Arrow Books)

Not only does the author clearly convey the American lilt in Scott Warrender's speech, she also effectively conjures up the period wartime feel in Poppy's responses and reactions.

There is a sense, too, of the characters circling round one another in a way that is typical when there is mutual attraction. Keen to get to know each other better, each one is anxious to sustain the moment and worried that they might say the wrong thing and miss the opportunity of a lifetime.

SWEARING AND SLANG

Whether or not a writer decides to use expletives depends not only on the style and content of the story but also on the author's own sensibilities. You may feel swearing is an integral part of your character's personality and without it, their dialogue would lack realism.

Used sparingly, swear words can add impact and pace to dialogue but gratuitous use of obscenities is offensive and unnecessary. Where a scene is violent or a character is depicted as being extremely angry, upset or frustrated, the occasional expletive will add realism and power to the scene. Too many obscenities will, however, have a diluting effect and the full impact will be lost.

Using slang

Slang dates very quickly so that a contemporary piece of fiction, liberally sprinkled with buzz words from up-to-the-minute speech, will appear quaint and odd in a few year's time.

Slang is, however, an invaluable method of conveying period. For example, can you date the following phrases?

1. She thinks she's the cat's pyjamas.
2. Right-on man – that's groovy.
3. You're doing my head in.

(Answers at back of book.)

The characters' ages play a large part in the use of slang. Different generations have their own slang languages and as we have seen, the most effective method of conveying a different language is through the use of the odd word here and there, rather than trying to reproduce it in large, indecipherable chunks.

Writing dialogue is not so much a matter of reproducing exactly how people speak to one another in real life. It is more about setting down on the page a representation of speech which helps the writer convey character, period and plot in a realistic way.

CASE STUDIES

Elizabeth uses perfect English
Elizabeth is a retired English language teacher. After a lifetime of correcting her pupils' grammar, she finds it impossible to ignore the rules and allow her characters to speak naturally to one another. As a result, she is unable to develop clearly identifiable 'voices' for her characters and their dialogue is stilted and unrealistic.

Brenda acts out each situation
Brenda is a mother of four. Her children's ages range from 18

to 30. She is a keen amateur actress and member of her local drama society. She has a good ear for language and her family keeps her abreast of the latest slang phrases. Her interest in thriller writing means that she uses tough, uncompromising characters who have colourful vocabularies. She is not afraid to use expletives or slang in the right context. As a result, her writing is vibrant and realistic.

CHECKLIST

1. Do your characters each have their own distinctive 'voice'?

2. Can you tell who is speaking to whom by the dialogue alone?

3. Have you used a combination of dialogue and action?

4. Are you sure the dialogue is not stilted?

5. Have you been sparing with your use of slang and accents?

6. Does the dialogue move the story forward?

ASSIGNMENT

If you belong to a writing group, there is a simple exercise which demonstrates how a conversation develops.

Going clockwise round a circle, the first person begins with the phrase, 'I'm sorry, you can't have the car tonight', then turns to the next person for a response, which is usually, 'Why not?' Continue in this manner, making a rule that the dialogue must be brought to a satisfactory conclusion.

The end result will usually be a compromise between the two characters who have evolved. (Nine times out of ten, the dialogue develops into an argument between father and son.)

7

Finding True Love

WRITING A ROMANCE

A romance is the story of a man and a woman who meet and
fall in love against all the odds. The ingredients for a standard
romance are:

+ attractive central characters

+ a beginning, middle and happy ending

+ an element of suspense

+ obstacles designed to keep the hero and heroine apart

+ a satisfactory conclusion, culminating in the promise of
  marriage.

Romantic fiction is true escapism and great fun to write as
you steep yourself in a vision of what life could be like if only
all your dreams could come true.

Most but not all romantic fiction is written by women. This is
because it is centred around a particularly feminine, idealised
perception of what a loving relationship should be. The male
hero is strong, yet gentle. A caring, nurturing creature, who
puts the needs and desires of the heroine before his own.

Believe what you write

A tongue-in-cheek approach to romantic fiction simply won't work. In order to write convincingly, you must believe in your characters and be prepared to fall helplessly in love with the hero.

This doesn't mean you can't bring humour into the story. Providing you are laughing with and not at your characters, you can make them and their situation as amusing as you wish. At the end of the day, however, you have to care whether or not your characters proclaim their love for one another and achieve the happy ending that is an integral part of every romantic story.

FINDING FLAWS ATTRACTIVE

Bearing in mind that attractive characters are central to the romantic theme, we need to explore the idiosyncrasies of sexual attraction.

Beauty in the eye of the beholder

It is tempting to depict your heroine as exquisitely beautiful – shining hair, immaculate complexion and a figure any woman would die for.

Equally, you might initially portray your hero as a picture of masculinity. Tall and handsome, with a head of thick, luxuriant hair and of muscular, athletic build.

They both look and sound wonderful, have warm, caring dispositions and to all intents and purposes, are perfect. Too perfect. We ordinary mortals know we haven't a chance with people like this. They would never fall for little old us, so in order to make your romantic characters appear more believable and, more importantly, attainable, it is necessary to give them a flaw.

Falling for the flaw

The flaw may be physical, perhaps the heroine is a little too short, the hero just an inch or so too tall. Whatever you feel it takes to make them a bit more human than if they were perfectly proportioned.

However, a physical flaw, whilst useful, only offers part of the picture. A rounded character will also have an emotional hang-up. Perhaps they are stubborn, proud, impetuous or absent-minded. These are the sort of characteristics that will at first exasperate and subsequently attract one to the other.

OVERCOMING INSURMOUNTABLE OBSTACLES

In Chapter 3, we saw how important it is to include conflict in a story. The scenario illustrating the point had a beautiful young woman meeting and marrying the man of her dreams and living happily ever after.

Whilst this formula is the basis for a romantic story, on its own without any conflict, it offers no sustainable plot.

Preventing the characters from succeeding

Having created your almost perfect characters and set them against a suitably romantic background, it would be very pleasant to simply sit back and let nature take its course. Sadly, that's the last thing a romantic writer can do. The author's task is to come up with devious ways to prevent the hero and heroine from getting together until the last possible moment.

As we have already formed a picture of television news-reader Sally Blake, we can use her as a heroine for our romance. Taking the first CV, where she is the product of a broken marriage, with a disinterested stepfather and a spoilt half-sister, we know that she is scared of forming permanent relationships. However, we also know that she is ambitious so, for the purposes of our story, we will need to sabotage:

1. any attempt on her part to form a lasting relationship with the hero

2. any exciting new career prospects.

Getting to know the hero

Before we can devise a plan of obstacles to their love, we need to get to know the hero.

Like Sally, Nick will have one or two endearing personal quirks. Perhaps he rubs the bump on his broken nose when he's concentrating or the corner of his mouth twitches when he is amused.

He has probably been hurt by a woman in the past and his attraction to Sally will be in spite of a determination not to repeat the experience. It will be these traits which will make him irresistible to our heroine.

Jumping to the wrong conclusion

By drafting a plan of obstacles to the couple's romance, as shown in Figure 7, we can see at a glance how they will fit into the storyline.

One of the most effective obstacles is the romantic hero and heroine's unerring talent for jumping to the wrong conclusion, as shown in Frame 5.

1. Sally's relationship with married Mark is rocky. Sally tells Mark they are finished. She meets Nick, a new cameraman.	2. Nick asks her out. She refuses. Mark offers her promotion on condition that she continues their affair.	3. She is level-headed in a crisis. She tells Mark she needs time to think. She bumps into Nick as she leaves the building. He senses something is wrong. They go for a drink.
4. Despite her problems, Sally finds herself falling for Nick. He takes her home and stays the night. He persuades her to stand up to Mark.	5. The following afternoon Sally overhears Nick deep in conversation with Mark. She mistakenly believes they are conspiring against her.	6. Sally fights with Nick, refusing to listen to his explanation. She resigns and walks out. At home, the phone rings constantly but she ignores it.
7. Job and romance prospects gone, Sally goes to stay with her mother in France. Sophie is spiteful and Sally miserable.	8. Nick arrives in France. A studio is looking for an 'anchor' for the main news. This was what he'd been discussing with Mark, trying to persuade him to let Sally go.	9. Everything is wonderful. Sally is in love and plans to return to the UK and take up the new job. Then she sees Nick going into Sophie's room.
10. Nick denies being in Sophie's room but in the middle of a romantic meal with Sally, Sophie bursts in screaming. Nick bustles her outside and into his car and they drive off.	11. Hurt and angry, Sally returns immediately to the UK and throws herself into her new job. She manages to break the hold Mark has over her but she can't get over Nick. Then, she sees him in the studio.	12. At first, she resists his attempts to talk to her until Sophie arrives and confesses that Nick was helping her kick her drug habit. Finally, Sally realises she can trust Nick and they confess their love.

Fig. 7. Plan of obstacles to romance (based on Figure 4). Sally ends affair with Mark and falls in love with Nick. Her emotional background prevents her from embarking on a new relationship. Finally, Nick wins her over and they achieve the requisite happy ending.

Sally's immediate reaction when she discovers Mark and Nick in conversation is to assume they are plotting against her. It never occurs to her that Nick might be trying to help her but if it did, she would thoroughly resent his interference. Either way, he cannot win.

The next misunderstanding occurs in Frame 10, with Nick's attention to Sophie. It is her fear of losing him to her spiteful step-sister that prompts Sally's ill-judged behaviour. Meanwhile, it is a combination of pride and integrity on Nick's part which governs his reactions.

Remember that, however many obstacles we throw in her path, Sally must have overcome them by the end of the book.

DRIVING FAST CARS AND WEARING FANCY CLOTHES

Romance and glamour go hand in hand and if you intend to write romantic fiction, you need glamorous settings for your stories.

Our story is set around the fast-moving background of a television news station. However, the worlds of high fashion, fast cars, thoroughbred horses and sporting champions also feature heavily in this kind of novel. No one wants to read about the love life of a garage mechanic and a secretary. Not, that is, unless the garage mechanic designs and builds revolutionary racing cars or the secretary works for a high-powered executive of an international industrial giant.

Following high fashion

Clothes are particularly important and always set off a hero's physique or a heroine's figure to perfection.

Even the poorest heroine seems to be able to lay her hands on at least one pure silk designer evening gown, whilst old, worn jeans and an open-necked work shirt enhance our hero's hard-man image as much as the cultured side of his nature is improved by his appearance in an immaculate tuxedo.

Keeping up with the times
In line with the glamour/power image, today's romantic heroine may well be in her mid to late twenties and running her own business. She may drive a powerful car, pilot a plane, sail a yacht or be an expert horsewoman and will not appreciate being treated as if she's a rare and fragile flower.

ENJOYING SEX AND FOOD
The only rule relating to the inclusion of sex in a romantic story is that it must be integral to the storyline and portrayed within the context of a love scene. Gratuitous sex, particularly if linked with violence, is totally unacceptable.

Practising safe sex
Some romantic writers always include explicit sex scenes, others never do. It is entirely up to you to decide whether or not you are comfortable writing about sex.

All sexual encounters between the hero and heroine are immensely pleasurable and safe sex is practised. This is all part of the caring, nurturing role which is the essence of the true romantic hero.

Eating and drinking sensuously
Eating is almost as important as sex in a romantic story. Meals are described in great detail and range from plain

but wholesome simple fare to delicately presented gourmet dishes.

For example, a romantic ploughman's lunch for two would consist of a fresh, French loaf, deliciously crusty on the outside, the soft, white middle thickly spread with creamy butter. The cheese will be firm and mature, served with a generous helping of tangy, home-made chutney. The whole thing will be washed down with a named wine, a fruity red or light, refreshing white.

Listed below is a selection of key words for describing food and drink:

cool	piquant
crisp	refreshing
crunchy	smooth
crusty	succulent
fresh	tangy
frothy	velvety
melting	

HEIGHTENING ALL THE SENSES

As we have seen in previous chapters, in order to bring fictional characters to life, it is important to bring all five senses into play.

In romantic fiction, these senses are heightened for maximum stimulation. Cars go faster, food tastes better, clothes feel silkier and voices are softer and warmer.

Things look better, too. Cars gleam, meals are feasts for the eyes, garments cling in all the right places, hair and eyes shine and flash, skin and muscles are soft or hard to the touch.

BRINGING THE HERO AND HEROINE TOGETHER

With all these sensations to look forward to, it's not surprising that romance is such a popular form of fiction. All that remains now is to bring our hero and heroine together.

In a romance, when hero and heroine meet, their first emotion should be any one of the following:

◆ anger
◆ dislike
◆ suspicion
◆ distrust
◆ intimidation
◆ embarrassment
◆ fear
◆ caution
◆ irritation
◆ reluctant attraction.

What it should never be is 'love'. That would be too easy and as we know, without conflict, there is no story.

HISTORICAL SETTINGS

The advantage of a contemporary romance is that you are writing about today's characters and can set them against backgrounds with which you are familiar. As we saw in Chapter 4, it is important to have accurate knowledge of a location whether it is a small provincial town or an exotic South Sea island. Background information must also be accurate. Knowledge of the television industry would, therefore, be essential for anyone writing Sally and Nick's story and for historical romances, accuracy is equally important.

Researching the period

For an historical story to work effectively, the right monarch must be on the throne and costumes, furnishings, vehicles, dialogue, attitudes and behaviour must all reflect the right period.

Romantic etiquette through the ages is a complex area. In order to write believable historical fiction, it is essential that the author understands and is thoroughly conversant with the conventions and rules of the period.

Employing the language of fans, for example, is one method by which a heroine could embark on a romantic liaison with a potential suitor. Like every other language, however, you have to know it to speak it.

You also need to know who would be deemed an unsuitable marriage partner and who would be considered an excellent catch according to the conventions of the time. Methods of overcoming parental opposition, schemes for bettering themselves or plans for eloping must all be workable within the context of the historical setting you have chosen.

Attending banquets

Eating and drinking was just as important in the past, if not more so. For the historical novelist, it is vital that you know what food was served and how it was cooked.

Finance also rears its ugly head as, whilst the hero and heroine will care nothing for monetary gain, financial status will have enormous implications on any potential marriage plans.

In romantic fiction, the background is as important as the plot and accuracy provides an ideal balance for the escapist tale you long to tell.

CHECKLIST

1. Would you fall in love with your hero?

2. Is your heroine attractive to both men and women?

3. Do you want them to live happily ever after?

4. Does your story have a happy ending?

5. Is the background information accurate?

6. Have you used all five senses effectively?

7. Is sex portrayed within the context of a loving relationship?

ASSIGNMENT

Select one of the following pairs and write the scene of their first meeting, conveying their reactions through a combination of dialogue and action:

◆ A male lawyer whose brilliance in court led to a miscarriage of justice against the young woman's father.

◆ A female hospital administrator charged with cutting costs and a male paediatrician.

◆ A minor lady-in-waiting at Queen Elizabeth I's court and a Spanish courtier.

8

Haunting, Thrilling and Killing

INTRODUCING A NOTE OF SUSPENSE

For some writers, the thrill of the chase has little to do with love. Their preference is for ghost and horror stories and the opportunity they offer to take their writing to the limits of their imagination.

Explaining the inexplicable

Ghosts take many forms and appear in novels in a range of guises and moods. They may be:

- friendly
- hostile
- sad
- happy
- mischievous
- malevolent
- humorous
- helpful
- obstructive
- manipulative
- powerful
- possessive
- terrifying
- comforting.

In addition to all those qualities, the form they take could be:

- a restless spirit
- a contented resident
- a poltergeist
- a messenger from the past, present or future.

Some ghosts assume clearly visible human form, others are opaque and some are simply a shapeless presence but the one thing they usually have in common is the ability to materialise and disappear at will.

Digging up the past
Ghostly characters are no different from any other protagonists and should be treated accordingly.

You need to dig deep into their past so that their background offers an excellent reason for their current existence. Their past will also explain their attitude to the mortals they encounter.

For the mortal characters, whether the ghost is frightening or friendly, the initial meeting must have an element of suspense – a creaking floorboard, sudden icy draught, a slamming door or window.

CONFRONTING THE FEARS WITHIN
Whilst not every horror story features a ghost, the two genres often overlap as both set out to frighten the reader.

Horror stories exploit our fears and shock us into facing the thing we believe to be lurking in the shadows. If you are frightened of spiders, for example, it's bad enough if you see one crawling up your arm. Imagine how much worse it would be if you were locked in a dark room with dozens of them running around you. You might not be able to see them but you'd certainly know they were there.

In fact, they need not be there at all, you simply have to believe they are and your imagination will do the rest for you. Before long, you'll start to feel them crawling up your legs and over your body.

Confronting your worst nightmare

Horror fiction is based on the principle of confrontation with your worst nightmare and common phobias are used to great effect in both ghost and horror stories.

The prospect of spending the night in a haunted house, for example, mercilessly exploits our natural fears of the dark and isolation. Among the spooky sensations and incidents guaranteed to scare us silly are:

◆ being cut-off from the outside world

◆ lack of warmth and light

◆ no visible escape route

◆ having supporting characters mysteriously disappearing one by one.

Losing control

The underlying theme of the scenarios featured above is that of powerlessness.

Once a character is trapped in a situation, they must rely heavily on their wits for survival and if they've had those wits frightened out of them, we won't hold out much hope for their chances.

Loss of control or free-will is another very powerful theme in ghost and horror stories and includes:

* being under attack from monsters, e.g. werewolves, vampires, zombies etc.

* being trapped alone with your worst nightmare

* having your mind and/or actions controlled by someone evil

* being unable to find an escape route, i.e. every road you take leads back to where you started

* being unable to distinguish between reality and falsehood, i.e. are you insane?

* being the only one to recognise the growing danger, i.e. being quite alone.

CONTRASTING NORMALITY WITH TERROR

Contrasting fear of the unknown with a background of familiarity produces an immensely strong feeling of terror and suspense.

Creating an element of doubt

Picture a scene of contented domesticity. A housewife is tackling the routine chores when the phone rings. Just as she is about to pick up the receiver, it stops. Nothing particularly unusual here, just a wrong number. Unless, of course, the same thing happens continually throughout the day.

By the time her husband returns home from work, our house-wife is a bundle of nerves. He manages to calm her, putting it down to phone engineers working on the line.

That evening they are watching TV when the wife hears a noise outside. Husband investigates but can see nothing. The cat strolls in through the open door and they laugh the incident off.

In bed that night, the wife is woken by the phone ringing. Her husband stirs but doesn't waken so she makes her way down-stairs to answer it but when she picks up the receiver, the line is dead. She returns to the bedroom and climbing back into bed, snuggles close to her husband but something doesn't feel right. She tries in vain to rouse him and discovers he is dead, his face a contorted mask of fear.

Providing an explanation

Lull the reader into a false sense of security by providing credible explanations when the strange events begin so that, when the terror is revealed, it scares them as much as the central character.

Just when you thought it was all over

Depending on the style of the story you are writing, it is sometimes possible to add even more impact to the tale by reviving the monster just long enough for one last attack.

The central character has fought and vanquished his foe and is feeling justifiably euphoric. Nothing can harm him now, the town/city/world is saved and life is rapidly returning to normal.

Just when you thought it was all over, however, whatever grisly being is left after our hero has finished with it hauls itself painfully back from the dead and makes one last, usually unsuccessful, lunge towards him.

Laying the foundation for a sequel
Alternatively, as you approach the end of your novel, you may already be thinking about a sequel.

If so, it helps to give a hint that the means are there to recreate the terror. A flicker of life in a twitching limb, an unnoticed pod or egg, an indication that the conditions which gave rise to the terror could be reproduced if certain conditions were recreated.

WRITING A MURDER MYSTERY
Whilst murders frequently take place in both ghost and horror stories, we can derive comfort from the fact that the perpetrators are products of the author's vivid imagination.

The mortal murderer is a very different kettle of fish as he or she may be based on a real person or event.

Avoiding true stories
All writers exploit information gleaned from the media but care must be taken to protect innocent victims of true-life crime. The discovery of a murder victim's remains or an old newspaper cutting might trigger your imagination but for the families of those involved, it is a trauma from which they will never fully recover. By all means use true-life cases as a

framework for your stories but the background, characters and plot should be your own fictional creation.

Employing an amateur detective

For today's crimewriter, the gifted amateur detective in the style of Agatha Christie's Miss Marple is a thing of the past.

Nowadays the amateur is usually someone who happened to be in the wrong place at the wrong time. Having stumbled across a crime, they become entangled in the events which follow and are forced to solve the mystery in order to extricate themselves from the situation.

The attitude of the professional policeman in all of this is either one of outright hostility or downright suspicion. Indeed, our unwilling sleuths could well find themselves on the run from the law and unable to convince anyone of their innocence.

Consulting a specialist

Novels featuring amateur detectives are usually set against specialist backgrounds reflecting areas of their authors' own expertise. Ellis Peters' medieval monk, Brother Cadfael, for example and Jonathan Gash's roguish antiques dealer Lovejoy are just two such successful fictional sleuths.

In this type of novel, the fascinating backgrounds give rise to sub-plots and back stories which are as gripping to the reader as the crime being solved. If a new specialist amateur sleuth is to break into this overcrowded field of fiction, their background must be completely different from any other detective series currently on the bookshelves.

Relying on the professionals

'Police procedurals', where a professional police officer solves the crime, feature up-to-the-minute police methods and the latest advances in forensic science. Accuracy is vital and the detective needs to be a fairly colourful or eccentric character.

CHOOSING A MURDER WEAPON

The choice of murder weapon should be realistic, bearing in mind that the cause of death could be any one of the following:

- a blow from a blunt instrument
- stabbing with a knife or sharp implement
- poisoning
- shooting
- drowning
- strangulation
- suffocation.

Killing effectively

Whichever weapon and method you select, you must be sure that it will work and know what effects it will have on your victim. For example, if you intend to stab, shoot or physically attack your victim, could you answer the following questions?

- How much blood will there be?
- What shape will the wound be?
- How much force will be needed for the blow to be effective?
- How long will the victim take to die?

Poisoning the victim

Poisoning the victim's food is a favourite method but here again, it is imperative that you know a few basic facts:

- Is the poison easily detectable?
- Does it have a distinctive taste/odour?
- What quantities are you likely to need?
- Is it readily available and obtainable?
- What symptoms will the victim display?
- How long will the victim take to die?

Killing by accident

Occasionally a victim is killed by accident. They may fall down rickety steps and break their necks, have something heavy fall on them or be locked in the cellar of an empty house.

Under these circumstances, they tend to be victims of their own evil plans, having hatched the plot and fallen into their own trap. Occasionally, however, they are innocent, their death leading to untold problems for the character who was instrumental in causing it in the first place.

When planning a murder, be absolutely sure of your facts and remember, the simpler the plan, the more likely it is to succeed.

Killing by accident

PLOTTING AND PLANNING

A plot is simply what happens in a story and plot development depends a great deal on your characterisation.

Your characters' reactions to a given situation will have a strong influence on your plot. In a family saga, for example, the story will be centred around one character's relationship with their family and the people they encounter as their tale unfolds.

In contrast, crime novels are centred around the solution of the crime so that, whilst it is essential to have a strong protagonist, the book must be carefully plotted in order to keep up the interest. Before you begin to write the book, you must be very clear where all the twist and turns, clues and red herrings will occur.

You should also take note of the following advice from crime-writer Susan Moody: 'You must play fair with the reader. No twin brothers produced in the last chapter. Share the clues with the reader, your job is to hide them as skilfully as you can.'

Planning your novel

No matter what the genre, you should always draft out a plan or outline which takes the work through from its beginning to its logical end.

This helps you to plot both the main theme and any sub-plots or 'back stories' within a flexible framework. As we saw with the plan of obstacles to Sally's romance in Chapter 7, far more is going on than just her love affair with Nick.

Each stage of the plot must be set out within the frame of a chapter-by-chapter outline, so that you can see at a glance exactly where and when each incident occurs.

Using the plotline from Chapter 3 where Sally accidentally kills Mark, Figure 8 shows the draft plan of a crime novel. As you can see, the detail is very sketchy. At this stage the back story, or sub-plot, has been omitted but there will be room within each frame to slot in details of Nick and Sally's romance from our original plan.

An outline should be regarded as a flexible tool, which may be altered and shaped to suit the circumstances. You have to be comfortable with the idea of changing it round, taking some bits out and moving others to more logical places.

Devising a storyboard
Putting it on computer gives you the freedom to alter it at will although it does help if the plan is in constant view in storyboard or chart form while you are working. Some authors use wipe-clean boards or self-adhesive notelets which can be moved around and discarded when necessary, whilst others prefer a large sheet of white paper, drafting the plan out in pencil, colour coding, erasing or crossing out items where necessary.

Whichever method you select, once you have a plan to which you can work, it is much easier to slot in the plot changes when and where they occur and build up a visual picture of the completed novel.

Chap 1	Chap 2	Chap 3
Sally returns to flat to find Mark in foul temper. She says their affair is over, has met Nick. Ends with Mark's attempt to rape her.	Sally fights Mark off and he leaves. Later in bed is woken by phone. It's Nick. Mark has attacked him. He comes over. Love scene. Doorbell rings. Police. Mark is dead, killed by blow from paperweight from Sally's office desk.	Insufficient evidence to hold Sally. In office, papers re drugs story she was working on are missing. She hears noise, sees Nick rifling through Mark's desk and finding file. Confronts him, his story is lame, distracts him. Ends with her grabbing file and running.
Chap 4	**Chap 5**	**Chap 6**
Sally on Channel Tunnel train. Thinks she sees Nick but it is a lookalike. Relaxes, studies file, find links with both Mark and Nick. Ends with her leaving train unaware she is being followed.	At mother's house in France. Claude behaving strangely. Sophie looks pale and ill. Sally discovers Claude searching her things. They argue. She decides to return to UK. Ends with her seeing Nick in garden with Sophie.	Sally confronts Nick. Did he murder Mark? He swears his innocence. Says he was working on drugs case for rival news station. Love scene. Ends with Sally waking to find Nick, Sophie and file have all disappeared.
Chap 7	**Chap 8**	**Chap 9**
Sally returns to UK and studio. Checks computer, finds contact address in drugs case. Breaks in but is captured. Recognises major drugs baron. Ends with Nick arriving, revealed as gang member.	Sally in locked room. Hears scuffle outside. Sophie high on drugs pushed in, door locked. Sophie confesses she is a 'mule' (carrier) for the drugs baron. She is terrified of someone. Ends with failed escape attempt.	Sophie suffering withdrawal. Door opens, it is Claude, followed Sophie. Rescues girls but insists unsafe to go to police. They return to Sally's flat. Ends with her discovering it ransacked.
Chap 10	**Chap 11**	**Chap 12**
Sally begs Claude to call police. He refuses. She tries to call an ambulance for Sophie but he says he will get a doctor. Ends with Sophie trying to warn Sally about something but before she can name names, Nick arrives.	Nick agitated. Grabs Sally, she grapples with him, manages to escape, runs straight into Claude who brings her back inside. He confronts Nick, both men accuse each other.	Which man can Sally trust? She appears to choose Claude but he gives himself away by telling her how Mark was killed (couldn't know this). Fight. Nick saves them – reveals he is detective working undercover. Ends with promise of romance.

Fig. 8. Outline for crime novel.

Avoiding errors

Another great advantage of producing a visual aid like this is that errors in the storyline can be detected at a glance.

If, for example, you have a character who was killed in Chapter 3 unaccountably turning up in Chapter 5, you can remedy this before you get too far into the book.

A written plan allows you to see where each character is at any given moment and to calculate how to move them from and to each location. It also prevents you forgetting any minor characters along the way.

TWISTING THE TALE

Every crime story contains an element of suspense, provided by the twists and turns in the plot.

Laying a false trail

Twisting the tale involves laying a false trail in such a way that any surprise ending is a feasible one. The clues must be double-edged, so that whilst carefully steering the reader in the wrong direction, on closer examination they actually lead to the right one.

For example, in our story about Sally Blake, the minute Nick meets Sophie, he appears to be following Route (a) in the chart in Figure 9, ditching Sally in favour of her sister when, in fact, he is actually following Route (b). As both routes are equally valid, neither Sally nor the reader will feel cheated when the truth is revealed.

Nick appears to be very interested in Sophie	(a) He finds her sexually attractive
	(b) He recognises that she is a drug addict
When questioned by Sally, Nick is evasive	(a) He wants to ditch her for her sister
	(b) He wants to protect her from the truth
Nick is cagey about his past	(a) He is a villain
	(b) He is a detective working undercover
Nick and Sophie disappear together	(a) They have run off together
	(b) Nick has taken her to a clinic to kick her drug habit

Fig. 9. Twist clue format. The reader should be deliberately led to believe that the first answers, Route (a) are correct. However, the second answers are equally valid and Route (b) is, in fact, the correct one.

In a twist story, the reader should be kept guessing right to the end. For detailed information on how to write twist-in-tale short stories, see my book in How To's Successful Writing series entitled *Writing Short Stories and Articles.*

Planting red herrings

Red herrings, unlike twists in the tale, are simply false trails which are designed to lead you down a proverbial blind alley. Each suspect is furnished in turn with an alibi and there is an element of challenge involved whereby the reader is being invited to unravel the mystery.

For example, Sally is initially the obvious choice for Mark's murderer but can be eliminated by a helpfully detailed pathologist's report.

This leaves us with the standard murder mystery question: 'if she didn't kill him, who did?' Nick, our next most obvious suspect, is released by the police, leaving us free to send the reader off on a number of false trails before the resolution of the mystery in the final chapter.

LOOKING TO THE FUTURE

Futuristic stories are enduringly popular and the science fiction writer can choose to write any of the following types of story, providing they are set against a scientific background:

◆ a romance
◆ adventure story
◆ political thriller
◆ psychological thriller
◆ murder mystery
◆ horror story.

Explaining the inexplicable

Unlike fantasy, which features magical creatures such as goblins and gremlins within parallel worlds and time zones, science fiction explores the concepts and implications of space and time travel, scientific developments and theoretical possibilities.

The premise you use need not be proven scientific fact but it must have a factual basis and it must be theoretically possible. Within these constraints, the science fiction writer can approach the genre from a variety of angles.

- Exploring the influence of technological change from both negative and positive angles.

- Voicing concerns for the future of the planet.

- Exploring the possible damaging effect of new technology when taken to the edges of theoretical probability.

- Using technological advances to provide a futuristic setting for an adventure story or political novel.

Recognising an alien

Aliens, like ghosts, can be hostile or friendly, depending on the tone of the story. Many are humanoid but if they are, they always have one strange characteristic by which they can be identified.

Of those that aren't humanoid, hostile aliens tend to be slimy or scaly, whilst friendly ones are usually cuddly and/ or furry. However, watch out for aliens disguised as earth creatures. These may take the form of insects or small mammals, only revealing their true identity under certain traumatic conditions.

Recognising an alien

As all aliens function differently from Earthlings, one effective method of introducing humour is to give your alien a slightly irritating quirk or habit which may or may not be the same as any special powers or abilities it may possess.

Travelling in time and space

Travel to the past often aims to prevent a catastrophe in the future or tackles political issues such as what might have happened if historical events had taken a different turn.

Travel to the future tends to explore the human potential for self-destruction, the effects of over-mechanisation, pollution and nuclear warfare.

Discovering new worlds

We now know so much about our own solar system that, if you wish to write about inter-planetary travel, you need to go much further afield.

Due to the vast distances involved, you have to find ways of preventing your characters from dying of old age before they reach their destination and there are a number of methods you can use:

- suspended animation

- deep freezing

- 'warp' speed drives for your spaceship

- 'hyperspace' – a dimension where distance is reduced to zero

- a 'generation' starship, i.e. a moving, living colony in space.

Losing sight of the story

Science fiction has so much to offer the writer in the way of technological background, exotic settings and political themes that it is all too easy to lose sight of the characters and plot.

In order to ensure that the setting does not swamp the story, follow the same rules that apply to every other form of fiction writing: well-drawn, believable characters and a story that is carefully planned and plotted from beginning to end.

CASE STUDIES

Bob loves to shock

Bob is a mature English Literature student. His special interest is horror and his writing is colourful and imaginative. Unfortunately, he is inclined to let his imagination run away with him, filling his stories with so much blood and gore that the shock effect he strives for is lost. Until he can tone down the imagery by taking a more subtle approach, he will fail to achieve his full potential as a horror writer.

Sue enjoys a good murder

Sue is a great fan of murder mysteries and her clerical job at the local police station has given her an excellent insight into police procedures. Drawing on the knowledge she has gained through her work, she is in the process of creating a female Detective Inspector and is currently planning a murder mystery novel featuring a back story dealing with sexual harassment within the police force.

CHECKLIST

1. Would your story allow a reader's imagination to play an

active role?

2. Have you written a chapter-by-chapter plan of your novel?

3. Have you charted the plot developments?

4. Have you thoroughly researched the background to your story?

5. If your story is based on true events, have you fictionalised the characters sufficiently?

6. Is your storyline credible and within the bounds of probability?

ASSIGNMENT

A teenage girl is babysitting for a couple new to the neighbourhood. She hears a noise upstairs, investigates but can find nothing amiss, the two children aged 3 and 9 are sound asleep. Continue this storyline, including the following points:

◆ other unusual events which occur throughout the evening

◆ an apparently innocent explanation of the noise

◆ a more sinister explanation of the noise

◆ the discovery of something relevant to the noise

◆ the implications to the girl and the family of this incident.

9

Writing for Children

THINKING BACK TO YOUR CHILDHOOD

For many novice writers, the desire to write for children springs from their enjoyment in making up stories for their own offspring.

Telling bedtime stories

Despite the influence of television and computers, bedtime in a comfortingly large number of families is still synonymous with storytime.

Parents still enjoy reading to their children, as they were read to when they were small and will jump at the chance to dig out their old favourites and introduce them to a brand new audience.

Telling bedtime stories

Sometimes, however, the stories need a little alteration. Perhaps the vocabulary is too difficult or the story rather frightening. We may feel a few changes are in order and before long, we are making up our own stories, replacing the leading characters with ourselves and our children.

Entertaining the family

Both child and parent gain a great deal from this exercise. The children enjoy being part of a nightly adventure and parents have fun letting their imagination run riot.

There may well come a point when an admiring relative or friend urges you to write these stories down and turn them into a book and if this is your intention, bear in mind that:

- Family stories usually include lots of little personal asides and 'in' jokes.
- The stories often feature incidents which are amusing only because they happened to family members.
- Telling stories to your own children is enjoyable because they understand and relate to your sense of humour.

Consequently, the very things about your stories which appeal to your own children may hold little or no interest for anyone outside your circle of family and friends.

Broadening your horizons

If you intend to write work of a publishable standard for children, you must considerably broaden your horizons.

Begin by exploring your attitude to children in general. If you love them all unreservedly, believing them to be delightfully angelic creatures, children's writing is probably not for you.

LOOKING AT LIFE THROUGH A CHILD'S EYES

In order to write effectively for children, you need to think and react as they do. To help you look at life through the eyes of a child, consider how a tiny baby functions within its environment. Under normal circumstances, a baby cries for the following reasons:

◆ hunger
◆ discomfort
◆ pain
◆ tiredness.

We learn how to stop the baby crying through a combination of instinct, trial and error.

Manipulating adults

At the same time, the baby also uses trial and error to manipulate the adults who pander to its every need.

It learns very quickly how to stimulate the desired response in its parents and understands all too well how to react in order to avoid certain situations. At a very young age, the baby will be capable of quite complex behaviour guaranteed to drive its parents to distraction.

It is at this point that the baby begins to form the very accurate opinion that adults are highly irrational creatures.

Thinking rationally

Children are refreshingly direct in their thoughts and actions. In contrast, adult behaviour can appear extremely irrational. For example, the person who praises you for drawing a picture on a blank sheet of paper will, for no reason immediately obvious to the average toddler, punish you severely for drawing a similar picture on a blank wall.

By the time the child is walking and talking, it knows that everything it does has a certain risk factor attached to it. When attempting something new, it runs a 50/50 chance of either being praised or getting into trouble.

Poking fun at authority

Once a child has begun to progress through the school system, it will begin to relate much more to slapstick humour, as demonstrated by the enduring popularity of comics such as *The Dandy* and *The Beano* (published by D. C. Thomson).

Children adore stories which poke fun at authority, an aspect of their nature which Roald Dahl, considered by some to be the greatest children's author of our time, shamelessly exploited.

Understanding how it feels

If you intend to write for children, you must be able to relate to their anti-authoritarian emotions.

There will be many significant incidents in your childhood that you have carried with you into your adult life. Try to remember exactly how you felt when they happened, what emotions you experienced and how long it took you to get over them.

It is surprising just how much stays with us into adulthood, especially if we have been at the receiving end of particularly spiteful or thoughtless behaviour.

Being small and powerless

The one emotion that is shared by all children is the feeling of powerlessness in the face of adult supremacy.

Looking at life through a child's eyes gives you a very different perspective from that of a grown-up. Adults can come and go as they please, buy what they like, eat what they like, do and say what they like and more importantly, they are big and powerful.

A child, on the other hand, is small and powerless, subject to the whims and wishes of pretty well anyone bigger than themselves. It is surely no coincidence that, as we saw in the previous chapter, the concept of being powerless is a recurring theme in horror stories.

Relating to the right age group

Before you attempt to write stories for children, decide which age group you relate to best. Children are as varied in their tastes and interests as adults but whilst there is no limit on the themes you can explore, vocabulary and style is a very different matter. As Margaret Nash, author of many children's books, including the popular 'Class 1' series, explains:

> Plots have to move much faster for children than adults and each chapter should include some particular interest as well as some form and progression.

Read with a writer's eye books written for the age group of your choice and in order to establish the vocabulary and concepts you should be using, study National Curriculum reading schemes.

If you can, offer your services to the local school as a volunteer helper and read stories to the children. During these story sessions, assess their reactions by noting the following points:

◆ How soon do they begin to fidget?
◆ Which stories hold their attention and which do they find boring?
◆ What type of story do they enjoy the most?
◆ Which stories stimulate reactions and why?

PLAYING AROUND WITH IDEAS

Take a good look at the latest children's books, particularly those which are recommended for use within the National Curriculum. You will find that they deal with a staggering variety of topics, ranging from serious lifestyle issues to fantasy adventures.

When writing for very young children, you need to use simple, basic concepts and familiar situations. As their social skills develop, humour plays a much larger part and includes slapstick, puns, one-line jokes and wisecracking characters.

Once the child approaches teenage, the range of topics matches that of adult material, the main difference being the fast-paced style, vocabulary and attitude. The teenage novel is a rapidly expanding market for authors who have the ability to identify with this difficult stage of a child's development.

WRITING FOR EDUCATIONAL MARKETS

Writing for children involves both entertaining and educating the reader and for non-fiction writers, there is a variety of opportunity to do just that.

Reading comics and magazines

Glancing through the wealth of comics and magazines on the newsagents' shelves, you will find something for all age groups and interests.

Newspapers and magazines occasionally feature pages for children and may take nature, craft or activity articles. One or two comics have joined forces with national organisations such as the **Brownies** who, along with many other national children's clubs and societies, produce their own magazine. A combination of specialist knowledge and the ability to write with the clarity required for a young readership could lead to a wide variety of outlets for non-fiction articles.

Educating young readers

Both non-fiction and storybooks for children offer enormous scope to teach young readers about the world around them. The following is just a taste of what can be covered:

◆ conservation and ecological issues
◆ engineering
◆ geography
◆ history
◆ information technology
◆ manufacturing
◆ science.

Bearing in mind the expertise required, the educational book market can be quite difficult to break into.

Harcourt Educational Publishers, the UK's leading publisher of educational materials, admits that very few of the hundreds of unsolicited manuscripts they receive each year are accepted. Almost all of the material they publish is specially commissioned from experienced educational authors.

However, if you really think you have something worth looking at, Harcourt has this advice for first-time authors:

♦ Familiarise yourself with the publisher's catalogue – it's no good sending your best poetry collection to a publisher that specialises in non-fiction.

♦ It may be worth talking to the publisher in advance, to find out their needs and current projects and see if what you propose fits in with their plans.

♦ Make sure you pitch your writing at the right level for the intended reader – remember that most educational publishers produce material for children to read themselves, not for adults to read to them.

♦ Think carefully about the age and interest levels of your reader, and choose the content of your writing accordingly.

♦ Demonstrate any experience you have of working with children, particularly if you have used the materials you want to publish.

♦ This may sound obvious, but to get noticed, you need an original idea! (The 'orphan becomes heroic wizard' plot line has been taken!)

'The biggest problem with most of the proposals we receive is that the writer has not thought properly about the reader,' says one of Harcourt's Primary Literacy Publishers. 'Adults tend to make assumptions about what children like to read about, and they usually plump for the "cutesy" topics for very young children – bunnies, bears, families of elves at the bottom of the garden. If the story is over 1,000 words long, the average reader will be about 7 or 8 years old – and unlikely to be interested in the adventures of Barney the Bunny.

'Our other problem is that we publish mostly large, and carefully structured reading schemes. Individual story submissions, or ideas for a small series of books, very rarely fit into our portfolio. But we are open to good ideas and just occasionally a story comes in that demonstrates real talent – it's really pleasing when that happens.'

Being politically correct

Political correctness is an increasing feature of all walks of life and as with all good intentions, the basic idea behind the principle is sound. In its best form, political correctness addresses, among other things, the attitudes and concepts which give rise to:

- racism
- sexism
- prejudice against people with disabilities
- the concept that a two-parent family with 2.4 children is superior to any other
- class prejudice.

What are little boys/girls made of?

Until relatively recently, most children's fiction traditionally depicted boys as the leaders, solving mysteries, forming gangs and generally running the show. Girls were grudgingly allowed to tag along in order to provide refreshments and be rescued whenever necessary.

Any strong-willed girls who understood anything mechanical or were in any way sporty were labelled 'tomboys' and never quite fitted in with the rest of the group.

School stories have always been and still are immensely popular but the school featured was invariably the boarding variety and very definitely upper middle class.

Changing times
Times have changed and thankfully, attitudes have moved on. Black, Asian and foreign characters are no longer portrayed as caricatures, whilst tough girls and sensitive boys are perfectly acceptable.

Today's publishers acknowledge that not every child comes from a two-parent family and that goodness and decency are not necessarily commensurate with a white, middle-class background.

The influence these positive changes in attitude have had on children's fiction should not be under-estimated.

Reflecting today's lifestyles and values
Modern children's fiction reflects today's lifestyles and values in a fast-moving, multicultural society.

In an age of interactive computers and the information superhighway, youngsters have never been so well-informed. The children's author of today keeps abreast of the latest technogical developments, is up-to-date with current school systems and relates to modern attitudes and concepts.

ANTHROPOMORPHISING ANIMALS
At first glance, 'anthropomorphising' or humanising animal characters would appear to be the ideal way to capture and hold a child's attention.

Change all the characters in your story to cuddly animals, dress them in picturesque clothes, place them in a country setting and you can forget all about modern technology, the kids will love them to bits.

Assuming a parental role

Anthropomorphised animals do, it is true, have instant appeal but they also perform a variety of other functions. They can be:

♦ adults that behave like children
♦ children with capabilities far exceeding their actual age
♦ naughty to make a moral point
♦ a metaphor for their human counterpart.

Having your animal playing the part of a silly adult offers the young reader the opportunity to feel superior and adopt the parent role. The naughty animal can get into all sorts of scrapes from which it has to be rescued, making a moral point in the process.

Your animal character may, however, be a child. In this case, it usually has skills, commonsense and abilities far beyond its true age but because it is an animal, this appears perfectly acceptable.

Animal characters can also be used to portray frightening or threatening concepts. The most familiar examples are, perhaps, the themes used in traditional folk tales such as the three little pigs and the big bad wolf. The moral messages are always there but are more palatable when delivered by animals rather than people.

Appealing to older children

There is no age limit for anthropomorphised animals. Books like *Watership Down* aimed at young teens to adults have a very powerful effect. The animal society they portray is a metaphor for its human counterpart and as such, complex issues can be dealt with in a way which will be readily absorbed by younger readers.

WRITING ABOUT CHILDREN

Attitudes in children's publishing have changed dramatically over recent years. Although animal stories continue to be popular, the majority of children's books today have a child as their central character.

Solving a problem

In the same way that conflict is an essential ingredient in adult fiction, giving your central character a problem to solve is the main concept behind any children's story.

The basic formula which can be applied to children's fiction is:

---

character – problem – solution

---

bearing in mind that the child central character must be the one to find the solution to the problem. It is tempting to produce a kindly adult to save the day but this would defeat the object of the exercise.

Providing the problem

As a general rule, adults in children's stories tend to be one or a combination of the following:

- stupid
- self-absorbed
- eccentric
- unhelpful
- downright nasty.

Their main function is usually to perform tasks that cannot be handled by the child characters, like operating heavy machinery or writing cheques, to provide the humour or to be rescued as necessary.

The adult character may also provide the problem to be over-come but is rarely of much practical use. Children need to be able to relate to the characters in their stories and allowing an adult to take control is tantamount to selling-out to the enemy.

WRITING PICTURE BOOKS

Picture books present a whole new set of challenges. The pictures may perform a variety of functions, depending on the type of book. They can:

- tell the entire story without any text at all
- provide an interactive dimension
- provide an educational element
- add to the tone (humorous, frightening, exciting etc.)
- complement the story.

In picture books for the very young, it should be possible for the child to understand what is happening purely from the pictures alone.

Moving up in age, the illustrations should complement the storyline, adding depth and dimension to the story and helping to bring the characters alive.

Finding an illustrator

It is not a good idea to draw the pictures yourself unless you are a trained illustrator. If the idea for your picture book is strong enough, a publisher will find a suitable illustrator for you.

Because the illustrations are so important, this may take some time, possibly years rather than months. Due to the skill and time involved in illustration, the artist often receives a higher payment than the author.

On the plus side, picture books are so expensive to produce that if your manuscript is accepted, you can be sure of the publisher's commitment to you and your work.

CASE STUDIES

Vic entertains his grandson

Vic is a retired journalist. His column ran in the local press for over twenty years but now he has time on his hands, he would like to try his hand at writing for children. He used to make up stories for his own children and enjoys retelling them now to his seven-year-old grandson but recently noticed the child's attention wandering. When questioned, the boy confessed that he found the stories old-fashioned and said he would rather be playing computer games.

Ben tries an experiment

Ben is a science teacher at a large comprehensive school. Utilising his knowledge of school systems and the National

Curriculum, he devises a plot in which a group of children working on a class project make an amazing scientific discovery. They show their teacher who promptly takes all the credit and the children have to combine forces to prove to the school's head that they are the true inventors of the formula. The vocabulary is correctly pitched and as they are based on Ben's own pupils, the characters are very realistic.

CHECKLIST
1. Have you identified the age group for which you wish to write?
2. Is your vocabulary appropriate?
3. Is your story told from a child's perspective?
4. Does your story reflect modern attitudes and lifestyles?
5. Will your story appeal to today's child?
6. Do your child characters solve the problem themselves?

ASSIGNMENT
We have all experienced similar incidents to those listed below:

- Your sibling got a present and you didn't.
- You got a present and your sibling didn't.
- You won a prize.
- A childhood illness caused you to miss a treat.
- You fell over and hurt yourself and everyone laughed.
- A much-loved pet died.
- You were hauled out of your desk at school and told off in front of the whole class for something you didn't do.

Think back to your childhood and write down the emotions you felt when such incidents occurred.

10

Sending Your Work to a Publisher

SEEING YOUR WORK IN PRINT

Surveys conducted by both the Workers' Educational Association and adult education authorities have shown that over 90 per cent of students enrol on creative writing courses with the intention of learning how to write for publication.

Unfortunately, the harsh realities of the publishing world can, for some, come as a terribly cruel shock.

Meeting the publisher's requirements

Creativity is, of course, a vital ingredient but even the most gifted writer will fail in their bid to achieve publication if they are unable to fulfil certain criteria. For example, the majority of mainstream newspaper and magazine editors expect to be able to contact you via both fax and email and the non-fiction articles and features you write for them to:

- be computer-produced in double-line spacing
- be written to the specified length
- cover previously agreed subject matter
- have a beginning, middle and an end
- arrive by an agreed deadline.

Fiction for magazines should be typewritten, preferably on a

PC, in double-line spacing on one side only of A4 white paper. On acceptance, you may well be asked to re-submit the story via e-mail or possibly on disk.

Creative writers who are prepared to comply with these criteria stand a much greater chance of finding markets for their work than those who never consider the practical requirements of writing for publication.

Finding the right market
The following magazines usually welcome good, reliable contributors:

◆ club
◆ company 'in-house'
◆ religious
◆ school
◆ special interest.

Useful market information, advice on writing techniques and news of developments in the publishing world can be found in a number of writing magazines. Subscription addresses are listed at the end of the book.

PLAYWRITING FOR YOUR LOCAL DRAMA GROUP
It is notoriously difficult for new playwrights to get their work performed in the legitimate theatre but if you are lucky enough to have a repertory theatre in your locality, keep an eye out for schemes designed to encourage new authors.

Regional Arts Councils occasionally sponsor competitions and drama projects and one or two leading playwrights run schemes for young writers. It is worth keeping your eyes and ears open for scriptwriting projects in your area.

Working with your local drama group

One way you may be able to see your plays performed is by contacting your local amateur dramatic company.

Published plays are subject to performing rights payments and this is an expense many amateur groups can ill-afford. Having a tame author who can keep them supplied with imaginative scripts is, therefore, a huge asset and provides the would-be playwright with a valuable training ground.

ENTERING COMPETITIONS

Competitions offer enormous opportunities for writers in every field of writing but perhaps most particularly in the women's magazine market where, for many winners, they can be the first step towards a career as a novelist.

Competitions are regularly listed in the writing press and often levy a legitimate entry fee of between £1 and £5, but be aware that some advertisements, particularly in national newspapers, can be misleading.

Paying for prizes

Poets find it especially difficult to find a publishing outlet for their work, so it is not surprising that they can fall victim to unscrupulous advertisers.

The prize is publication in an anthology which the so-called 'winners' are invited to purchase for anything from around £12 upwards. Knowing that few writers can resist the opportunity to see their work in print, the competition organisers can be sure of receiving at least one if not more orders from each entrant. The book, if it ever materialises, is generally poorly produced and contains few poems of any literary merit.

The writers' magazine *Writers News* has mounted a campaign against these competitions and refuses to feature advertisements for them. According to editor Richard Bell, competition winners should expect to receive a complimentary copy of any anthology containing their work or if this is not possible, it should at least be available in the library.

Selecting the sensible option
There are, however, plenty of reputable bodies running competitions which, depending on the rules, conditions and the prize on offer, may open useful doors for the winning author.

VANITY PUBLISHING
Despite all the warnings regularly given in the writing press, novice authors are still persuaded to part with money in order to see their work published in book form.

Paying for publication
The price for this dubious privilege may start at four figures and can escalate beyond your wildest imagination. Horror stories include tales of people selling their homes and everything they own in order to pay for something that is, as far as the commercial book world is concerned, completely worthless.

If you are driven by countless rejections from legitimate publishing houses to investigate the world of the vanity publisher, be aware that:

1. Their income is derived from being paid to produce a book. Once this part of the bargain is fulfilled, they have no need to waste any expenditure on marketing.

2. Vanity publishers are under no obligation to distribute the book and rarely have distribution outlets.

3. Books produced by vanity publishers usually look unprofessional and are easily identified by book retailers who will have little interest in ordering them.

4. The published books are legally the property of the publisher. Any payments you make are purely to cover the cost of production.

5. Remember the golden rule **publishers pay you**.

SELF-PUBLISHING

Self-publishing differs from vanity publishing in that the author sets up and controls the publication and marketing of their book.

This involves paying a printer, finding retail outlets and handling all the distribution and publicity. It is, therefore, imperative that before you embark on the expense of publishing your own book, you are quite sure that there is a market for it.

Finding a gap in the market

The majority of successful self-published books are non-fiction and invariably fill a gap in the market.

For example, your business may involve travelling around the country but as you work for yourself, your budget may be very tight. Perhaps you have built up a personal directory of B & B establishments offering exceptionally good value for money. So many of your colleagues ask to borrow your directory that you realise it has potential as a saleable commodity. You obtain quotes from local printers and choose the one which will give you the best result at a realistic price.

The advent of desk-top publishing has helped to bring production costs down, so this may not be too prohibitive, but distribution can still be a problem. Retail outlets are unenthusiastic about taking self-published books, so you should consider setting up a mail order operation. Advertise in the appropriate trade press and on the Internet and providing you do not expect the project to make you either rich or famous, it can prove to be a very satisfying exercise.

Selling your idea

Before you embark on the expense of publishing your own non-fiction book, however, it is worth trying a professional publishing house.

Publishing made easy

It is worth noting that the combination of desk-top publishing and the Internet has brought about a major change to the image of self-publishing.

Rather than cope with organising the production and marketing of your book yourself, you may be tempted by the many advertisements for self-publishing companies in the writing press and on the Internet.

In addition to publishing, the services on offer range from critiquing, editing, design and publicity to marketing and

Internet sales through their own online bookshops. Some even offer advice on arranging book launches and bookshop signings and guarantee you distribution through online bookstores such as Amazon.com. Book lists and resumés of their existing authors may be readily available on their websites, together with submission guidelines for would-be authors.

However, if you are considering 'self-publishing' your manuscript through one of these companies, it is imperative that you check their credentials carefully to ensure that they are not simply vanity publishers in an updated, online form.

If your idea is good enough and you are convinced that there is a market niche for it, then your first step should always be to contact a suitable publisher. Market research is essential in order to help you familiarise yourself with the structure and length of similar books. Try to find a series into which your topic will fit, then write a chapter-by-chapter outline along the lines illustrated in Figure 10.

When you are sure that you have sufficient material to sell your idea, make a list of suitable publishers and telephone or write an initial enquiry letter asking if they would be prepared to consider your proposal.

If the idea is strong enough, you will be asked to submit your written outline based on the publisher's house style. Reputable publishers will usually respond quite quickly, probably within 4–6 weeks. Any longer than three months and you should chase them up and if necessary, request that the outline be returned to you (see Figure 11).

INTRODUCTION

CHAP 1: CHEAP AND CHEERFUL ACCOMMODATION
Under £15 per night
Off-road parking
Near town centre
Close to motorway

CHAP 2: THREE STAR AND OVER
En suite rooms
Full English breakfast
Special deals
Extra facilities

CHAP 3: LONG-HAUL STOPOVERS
Lesser-known routes
Farmhouses
Warm welcomes
Value for money

CHAPTER 4 ONWARDS: continue in this format until the last chapter which, for this type of book, would be along the following lines:

COSTS AND RECORD-KEEPING
Comparison of costs and services
Expenses, record-keeping, tax implications
Maps
Useful addresses

Glossary

Index

Fig. 10. Sample outline for non-fiction book.

ADDRESS, Tel/Fax/Email

date. . . . .

A Smith
Publisher
London W1

Dear Mr Smith

Following our telephone conversation in January this year, as
requested I submitted an outline for THE SALESMAN'S B & B
DIRECTORY.

It is now three months since I heard from you and I would be
grateful if you could let me know whether you are interested in
publishing the book. If not, I would appreciate its prompt
return so that I may submit it elsewhere.

Thanking you in anticipation.

Yours sincerely

A Writer

Fig. 11. Sample chase-up letter.

WRITING A SYNOPSIS

A synopsis of a novel is a resumé of the book's story. Leading literary agent, Blake Friedmann, issues clear guidelines to authors on how to write a treatment or synopsis. They recommend that it is broken down into four sections:

1. **Introduction** – a brief selling statement about the book.

2. **Character biographies** – short biographies of all of the major characters.

3. **Statement of intent** – why you wanted to write the novel and whether it is based on a factual event.

4. **Synopsis or treatment** – a step-by-step storyline of the novel.

The guidelines explain that the synopsis conveys the emotion, not just the plot, by making it clear what motivates your characters and the impact of events on them.

Whilst all of the above information should be included, it is imperative that you keep your synopsis as brief as possible. Remember, its purpose is to capture a publisher's attention and hold it right through to the end.

Giving away the ending

One recurring error that irritates publishers and agents beyond belief is the synopsis which promises wonderful things but finishes with something like:

> 'If you want to know what happens next, you'll have to read the book!!!!'

Sadly, they won't. They'll probably just heave a sigh and send your manuscript back in the next available post.

Your synopsis is your sales pitch and should contain all your manuscript's strongest points, including details of a satisfactory ending.

PRESENTING YOUR MANUSCRIPT

There is no absolute rule about what you should send to either a book publisher or an agent but unless stated otherwise, it is generally a synopsis and three chapters.

Submitting user-friendly manuscripts

One of the first questions students on my creative writing courses ask is 'Do I have to type my manuscript?'

Handwritten manuscripts are almost always returned unread so, if you want to be published, your manuscript must be typewritten in double-line spacing on one side only of A4-sized white paper.

The equipment you use is a matter of personal preference but if you intend writing for mainstream magazines or newspapers on a regular, professional basis, then being user-friendly takes on a whole new meaning.

Unless otherwise stated, fiction manuscripts should still be submitted on A4 white paper as above, but once a short story has been accepted for publication you may be asked to resubmit it via email or on disk. It is rarely financially viable for you to pay someone to transcribe it for you so the initial outlay for a PC can prove an excellent investment.

Technophobic article writers, on the other hand, can face real problems as magazines and newspapers tend to look to electronic communication for their topical features. Many mainstream publications now ask would-be contributors to fax them with an idea and a working outline, rather than posting a completed manuscript. Regional newspapers may well request that contact is made via email.

Whilst there is still plenty of opportunity in the huge range of smaller, specialised publications, ambitious article and short story writers cannot afford to bury their heads in the sand and ignore the impact of the Internet on the mainstream publishing industry. For more information on writing for the mainstream market, see my book *Writing Short Stories & Articles*.

Removing staples and pins
Never use staples or pins to fasten the pages of your fiction manuscript. One of the quickest ways to annoy an editor is to wound their fingers on spiteful fasteners.

Another sure-fire irritant is the clear plastic folder, whose slippery surface can be almost guaranteed to send a pile of manuscripts crashing to the floor the minute anyone walks past the editorial desk.

Thinking ahead
Every editor, publisher and agent has a 'slush pile', a pile of unsolicited submissions which have to be read.

In order to ensure that your manuscript finds it way fairly quickly to the top of the pile, here are a few simple tips:

1. Include a brief covering letter and front sheet with each manuscript as shown in Figures 12 and 13.

2. Number each page consecutively.

3. Head each page with your name and the title of the manuscript.

4. Finish each page with 'm/f...' or 'cont/d.' to indicate more is to come.

5. End the final sheet with the word 'End' or a line of asterisks.

6. Manuscripts should be posted, unfolded in a large envelope.

7. Place book manuscripts unbound in a card folder or box.

8. Never fasten your manuscript with pins or staples.

9. Always attach sufficient postage to cover the full cost of returning your manuscript.

10. Attach a return envelope for the editor's reply but do not insist on having rejected articles, features or short story manuscripts returned to you. Editors will appreciate the fact that you are content to run off further copies from your PC.

APPROACHING AN EDITOR

One of the most frequent disappointments for new writers is having their manuscript returned with a standard rejection letter.

The rejection itself is disappointing enough but authors, keen to know where they are going wrong, long for a few

```
ADDRESS , Tel/Fax/Email

                                              date.........

A Smith
Fiction Editor
The Magazine
London W1

Dear Mr Smith

Please find enclosed a short story of approximately 1,000 words
entitled 'Acceptance' which I hope you will find suitable for
publication in The Magazine.

I have enclosed return postage for your convenience and look
forward to hearing from you in due course.

Yours sincerely


A Writer
```

Fig. 12. Sample covering letter.

```
          REAL NAME, ADDRESS, Tel/Fax/Email


                        ACCEPTANCE
          A short story of approximately 1,000 words
                            by
                  A Writer (or pseudonym)
```

Fig. 13. Sample front sheet.

pearls of wisdom from the publishing establishment.

Giving encouragement

Editors are simply too busy to write personally to everyone who sends them a manuscript but if your work shows promise, some will take the time to scribble a few brief words of encouragement.

Some have two standard letters, one an outright rejection, the other rejecting the piece but asking to see anything else you write. If you receive the second type, send something else off without delay – your toe is in the door.

Occasionally, an editor will phone you, either to accept the piece or ask if you can alter it slightly. If you want to see your work in print, agree to any changes they suggest. You may not like amending your work but it will be worth it in the long run.

It is no good expecting busy editors to teach you your craft. It is up to you to develop the ability to assess your own work and approach the right market, so before you submit a manuscript:

♦ Research the market thoroughly to establish the publishers likely to be interested in your manuscript.

♦ Find out if the editor prefers initial approaches to be in the form of enquiry letters or is prepared to consider completed manuscripts.

♦ Establish the name of the person to whom you should address your manuscript.

◆ Allow six to eight weeks before you write a chase-up letter (Figure 11).

◆ Take any editorial advice you are offered and act on it.

Multiple submissions

Until recently, sending your manuscript simultaneously to more than one publisher was frowned upon by the industry.

Now, however, publishers recognise that having to wait months for an answer can be frustrating and are prepared to tolerate authors making multiple submissions providing this is stated in the covering letter.

Looking at it from the publishers' point of view, by submitting your manuscript to them, you are offering it for sale. If, when they agree to buy it, you tell them you've just sold it to someone else, they will be justifiably annoyed that you have wasted their time. This is not a good way to win friends in the publishing industry.

COPYRIGHTING AND SYNDICATION

As soon as you commit your work to paper, it becomes your copyright. You may then offer for sale any number of rights in that work for publication purposes, e.g.:

◆ First British Serial Rights (FBSR)
◆ foreign rights, i.e. French, German, American etc.
◆ specific rights for a set period
◆ all rights for all purposes.

Signing away your copyright

FBSR means that the purchaser has the right to publish the

manuscript once only in Britain. The same applies to first foreign rights but you can also sell second, third etc. rights. Broadcasting, film and, with the growth of the use of the Internet, electronic rights are also in demand.

The more times you sell a manuscript, the more complicated the copyright process becomes but think very carefully before agreeing to sell your work on an 'All rights for all purposes' basis as you will be signing away all ownership of your manuscript.

Copyright is a complex and specialised field and if you are at all concerned about the rights you are being asked to sell, you should consult an expert.

Getting an agent
Carole Blake, joint managing director of leading literary agency, Blake Friedmann, states that the main advantage of having an agent is that the author has someone on their side who will give them honest criticism that will improve their career prospects.

Blake Friedmann receives approximately 400 unsolicited manuscripts per month but, on average, takes on only three to six new authors a year. Like publishers, literary agencies specialise in specific publishing areas and once again, market research is imperative before making an initial approach. As a general rule, agents do not handle short story and article writers, who may be better served by a syndication agency.

Syndicating your stories
With a shrinking UK market for short stories, many writers

try their luck abroad and a reputable syndication agent can lighten the load considerably.

They will sell your story to as many markets as possible all over the world, keep a record of sales and save you both legwork and heavy postage costs.

In return, of course, they will take a percentage, so before you hand over your manuscripts, make sure the terms are agreed in advance and in writing. Reputable syndication agencies are listed in *The Writers and Artists Yearbook*.

KEEPING RECORDS

From the day you send your first letter to an editor, you should keep a record of when and where you sent it, whether it was published and if so, how much you were paid.

Informing the Inland Revenue

Once payments start coming in on a regular basis, it is imperative that you have a clear record of everything you earn from writing.

Bear in mind that all payments from publishing houses are put through their books so even if you don't inform the Inland Revenue about your new source of income, your name will eventually come to their attention.

Offsetting your costs against tax

You can offset the cost of materials such as paper, ribbons, ink cartridges, postage etc. against tax and, of course, capital expenditure such as PCs, desks and filing cabinets.

Keep receipts of everything you purchase and record all your income and expenditure. Suggested formats for record-keeping are illustrated in Figures 14 and 15.

There are a number of useful leaflets available from the Inland Revenue and your tax inspector will be prepared to advise you or you may prefer to engage an accountant. Shop around to establish how much you are likely to be charged and remember, accountancy costs can be offset against tax and will prove to be a very worthwhile expense when your work really begins to take off.

FINDING SUPPORT FROM OTHER WRITERS

Writing, we are constantly told, is a very lonely occupation even though the image this presents is actually very romantic.

There you are, just you, your PC and your characters. You've locked the door, taken the phone off the hook and disconnected the doorbell. There is nothing to prevent you from producing a masterpiece. Unfortunately, you can't think of a word to write.

Confronting writers' block

It is arguable whether writers' block actually exists or whether it is simply brought about by the provision of perfect conditions in which to write.

Like our fictional characters, we will strive to overcome any obstacle in order to fulfil our ambitions to see our work in print. Remove those obstacles and we immediately yearn for distraction.

Stationery	Postage	Telephone (Bus. prop. only)	Subscriptions	Motor & Travel (Bus. prop. only)	Use of home as office	Sundries	Capital expend.

Fig. 14 Suggested headings for expenditure record.

TITLE	FORMAT	PUBLISHER	AMOUNT £	DATE PAID
Brewing Real Ale	Article (1,000 words)	Brewer's Monthly	50	12.7.0X
Hopping Holidays	Interview – hop-picker (500 wds)	"	25	2.8.0X
Beer for the Connoisseur	Article (1,500 words)	Home Brew	100	11.10.0X
One for the Road	Short Story (1,200)	"	75	21.12.0X

Fig. 15. Suggested headings for income record.

We long to have someone to talk to, preferably a like-minded person from whom we can gain some positive feedback. We need other writers.

Joining a writers' circle
Fortunately, help is at hand in the form of writers' circles, conferences, seminars and courses.

Your local library should have details of writers' activities in your area and writing organisations will be only too pleased to add your name to their mailing lists. Societies and associations for writers are listed at the end of this book but for some excellent on-the-spot advice, here are some words of wisdom from established writing professionals:

◆ 'I look for a strong story with believable, interesting characters that I know I will be able to interest a publisher in. Most irritating are sloppy writing, author arrogance and incorrect assumptions about the trade.' (Carole Blake, agent)

◆ 'Don't just sit there – get on with it!' (Patricia Burns, novelist)

◆ 'If you don't enjoy what you are writing, no one else will.' (Martina Cole, novelist)

◆ 'Don't wait for inspiration to come. Sit down and write, however hard it is. The act of writing itself stimulates the creative flow.' (Michael Green, humorist)

◆ 'Write every day, even if it's only for an hour a day, keep one hour sacred. Do not wait for inspiration, you may wait in vain.' (Susan Moody, crimewriter)

♦ 'Make writing your top priority after family and moral obligations, making sure you spend a certain amount of time each week either writing or thinking your story through, even if it means evening work. Read your work aloud and check for pace etc.' (Margaret Nash, children's writer)

Forming your own group

Whilst family and friends can be wonderfully encouraging and supportive, feedback from other writers is invaluable. If all else fails and you can find nothing in your area, why not start your own writers' group? You'd be amazed at the number of people who have a manuscript tucked away and would welcome the opportunity to share their love of creative writing.

Glossary

Anthropomorphisation. Giving animal characters human characteristics.

Article. A factual piece written for publication in a magazine or newspaper.

Back story. Background storyline or sub-plot against which the main action is played out.

Cliché. Stereotype.

Conflict. Problems and emotions providing the obstacles to be overcome in a work of fiction.

Copyright. The legal ownership of publication rights in a piece of written work.

Dialogue. Conversation between characters.

Double-line spacing. Leaving a blank line between each type-written line on a page.

Fiction. A made-up story, not fact.

Flashback. A method of revealing background through snippets of information.

Genre. The literary category into which your work falls.

In-house magazine. Publications produced by companies for their employees containing items of news about staff and changes within the organisation.

Interaction. How characters react to the people, settings and objects around them.

Letter to the editor. Letter intended for publication on a magazine or newspaper's letters page.

Location. Where the story is set.

Motivation. The reasons for a character's behaviour and attitudes.

Mule. Someone who carries concealed drugs through customs for drug smugglers.

Multiple submission. Sending the same manuscript simultaneously to a number of different publishers.

Narrative style. Using a narrator to tell the story.

Non-fiction. Fact.

Outline. Flexible step-by-step plan of a manuscript.

PC. Personal computer.

Piece. An article intended for publication.

Plot. The plan of events running through a story.

Police procedural. A crime novel where the detective is a police officer.

Political correctness. The requirement that attitudes and vocabulary in your manuscript are not offensive with regard to race, sex, creed etc.

Potted history. Brief resumé of a character's background.

Protagonist. The main character.

Reader identification. Characters and situations which are instantly recognisable to your intended readership.

Red herring. Clue deliberately implicating the wrong suspect in a crime story.

Self-publisher. An author who publishes and markets their own book.

Short story. A work of fiction of less than 10,000 words.

Showing not telling. Using interaction rather than narration to depict the sequence of events in an article or story.

Slush pile. Collection of unsolicited manuscripts waiting to be read by an editor or agent.

Stereotype. A fixed image of specific groups based on age, sex, race, religion, social status etc.

Stringer. Contributor of items of news to a local newspaper.

Syndication. To offer manuscripts for simultaneous sale to publications worldwide.

Synopsis. A step-by-step resumé of a book's story.

Unsolicited manuscript. A manuscript submitted unrequested for a publisher or agent's consideration.

Vanity publisher. A company which will agree to publish your manuscript in return for payment.

Answers to Assignments

CHAPTER 5 – SUGGESTED REWRITE OF 'SHOWING' NOT 'TELLING' EXERCISE
Original

It had been raining hard for days. Water streamed from the gutters of every roof, pouring down windows, along pavements, running in fast moving rivulets along each road. Underneath the streets, torrents of water gushed and gurgled beneath the feet of the people hurrying along the shiny wet pavements, pushing and shoving one another in their haste to get out of the rain. Steel grey storm clouds gathered overhead, meeting one another head on in preparation for yet another downpour. It was very, very wet. (85 words)

Rewrite

It was the third time this week Claire has been soaked to the skin on her way to work and she'd had enough. Why, she wondered, did heavy rain bring out the worst in people? The way they pushed and shoved, it was as though they believed they'd dissolve if they got too wet. Anxiously, Claire lowered her umbrella to peer up at the sky. More grey clouds. Not a hope of a break in the weather. (77 words)

CHAPTER 6 – DATE THE SLANG EXPRESSIONS

1. 1920–30s.
2. 1960–70s.
3. 1980–90s.

Useful Addresses

Blake Friedmann, Literary, TV & Film Agency, 122 Arlington Road, London NW1 7HP. Tel: (020) 7284 0408. Fax: (020) 7284 0442.
Email: firstname@blakefriedmann.co.uk
Website: www.blakefriedmann.co.uk

The British Science Fiction Association Ltd (BSFA), Membership Secretary, Estelle Roberts, 97 Sharp Street, Newland Avenue, Hull HU5 2AE.
Email: bsfa@enterprise.net Website: www.bsfa.co.uk

Comedy Writers' Association UK (CWAUK), 44 Cherry Avenue, Swanley, Kent BR8 7DU. Contact: Mark Nicholson. Tel/Fax: (01322) 410742.
Email: info@cwauk.co.uk
Website: www.cwauk.co.uk

Crime Writers' Association of Great Britain, PO Box 6939 Birmingham B14 7LT. Contact: Rebecca Tope, Membership Secretary. Email: info@thecwa.co.uk
Website: www.thecwa.co.uk

Harcourt Education Ltd, Halley Court, Jordan Hill, Oxford OX2 8EJ. Tel: (01865) 310533. Fax: (01865) 314641.
Email: uk-schools@harcourteducation.co.uk
Website: www.harcourteducation.co.uk

National Association of Writers in Education (NAWE), PO Box 1, Sheriff Hutton, York YO60 7YU. Tel: (01653) 618429. Email: info@nawe.co.uk

Websites: www.nawe.co.uk www.artscape.org.uk

National Association of Writers' Groups (NAWG) Secretary, 40 Burstall Hill, Bridlington, E. Yorks YO16 6GA. Tel: (01262) 609228. Email: nawg@tesco.net
Website: www.nawg.co.uk

National Union of Journalists (NUJ), 308 Gray's Inn Road, London WC1X 8DP. Tel: (020) 7278 7916. Fax: (020) 7837 8143.
Email: info@nuj.org.uk
Website: www.nuj.co.uk

Romantic Novelists' Association (RNA), Contact: Hon. Membership Secretary, 38 Stanhope Road, Reading, Berks RG2 7HN. Website: www.rna-uk.org

Society of Authors, 84 Drayton Gardens, London SW10 9SB. Tel: (020) 7373 6642.
Email: authorsoc@writers.org.uk
Website: www.writers.org.uk/society

Society of Women Writers & Journalists (SWWJ), Membership Secretary: Wendy Hughes, 27 Braycourt Avenue, Walton-on-Thames, Surrey KT12 2AZ (sae for membership details).
Email: swwriters@aol.com
Website: www.swwj.co.uk

Women Writers' Network, 23 Prospect Road, London NW2 2JU. Tel: (020) 7994 5861.
Website: www.womenwriters.org.uk

Workers' Educational Association (WEA), National Office, Temple House, 17 Victoria Park Square, London E2 9PB. Tel: (020) 8983 1515. Fax: (020) 8983 4840.
Email: national@wea.org.uk Website: www.wea.org.uk

Writernet (formerly New Playwrights' Trust), Cabin V, Clarendon Buildings, 25 Horsell Road, London N5 1XL. Tel:

(020) 7609 7474. Fax: (020) 7609 7557.
Email: writernet@btinternet.com
Website: www.writernet.org.uk
Writers' Guild of Great Britain, 15 Britannia Street, London
WC1X 9JN. Tel: (020) 7833 0777. Fax: (020) 7833 4777.
Email: admin@writersguild.org.uk
Website: www.writersguild.org.uk

USEFUL WEBSITES

www.arts.org.uk
www.author-network.com
www.bbc.co/writersroom
www.booktrust.org.uk
www.dictionary.com/doctor
www.dir.yahoo.com/reference/dictionaries
www.liveliterature.net
www.writernet.org.uk
www.writers-circles.com
www.writewords.org.uk
www.yourdictionary.com

Further Reading

Aslib Directory of Information Sources in the UK.

501 Writers' Questions Answered, Nancy Smith, Piatkus.

Encyclopaedia Britannica 2000 (2004 available on DVD and CD).

Chambers Twentieth Century Dictionary (available on CD).

Collins Electronic English Dictionary & Thesaurus.

Directory of Writers' Circles, available from Oldacre, Horderns Park Road, Chapel-en-le-Frith, High Peak, Derbyshire SK23 9SY. Tel: (01298) 812305.
Email: oldacre@btinternet.com

How to Make Money Writing Fiction, Carole Blake, Boxtree Books.

How to Turn Your Holidays into Popular Fiction, Kate Nivison, Allison & Busby.

How to Write Horror Fiction, William F. Nolan, Writer's Digest.

How to Write Stories for Magazines, Donna Baker, Allison & Busby.

Oxford Dictionary of Quotations

Oxford Compendium 3.0 Series (CD includes Concise Oxford Dictionary, Oxford Thesaurus, Oxford Dictionary of Quotations & Modern Quotations).

Research for Writers, Ann Hoffman, A & C Black.

Roget's Thesaurus, Penguin Books.

The Bloomsbury Guide to Grammar, Gordon Jarvie.

The Craft of Writing Articles, Gordon Wells, Allison & Busby.

The Hutchinson Concise Encyclopedia, Century Hutchinson.

The Way to Write Novels, Paddy Kitchen, Elm Tree Books.

The Writer's Handbook, Macmillan.

Writers' and Artists' Yearbook, A & C Black.

Writers-circles.com Directory, Diana Hayden, 39 Lincoln Way, Harlington, Beds LU5 6NG. Tel: (01525) 873197. Email: diana@writers-circles.com Website: www.writers-circles.com

Writing for Magazines, Jill Dick, A & C Black.

Writing for Radio, Rosemary Horstmann, A & C Black.

Writing Step by Step, Jean Saunders, Allison & Busby.

How To Books on Successful Writing

Awaken the Writer Within, Cathy Birch (2nd ed.)

A–Z of Correct English, Angela Burt.

Handbook of Written English, John G. Taylor.

Publishing a Book, Robert Spicer.

Times of My Life, Michael Oke.

Write & Sell Your Novel, Marina Oliver (3rd ed.).

Writer's Guide to Copyright and Law, Helen Shay (3rd ed.).

Writer's Guide to Getting Published, Chriss McCallum.

The Writer's Guide to Research, Marion Field.

Writing a Children's Book, Pamela Cleaver (3rd ed.).

Writing Short Stories & Articles, Adèle Ramet (3rd ed.).

Writing Your Life Story, Michael Oke.

Magazines for writers

The New Writer, POB 60, Cranbrook, Kent TN17 2ZR. Tel: (01580) 212626. Fax: (01580) 212041. Email: editor@thenewwriter.com

Website: www.thenewwriter.com

Writers Forum, Writers International Ltd., PO Box 3229, Bournemouth BH1 1ZS. Tel: (01202) 716043. Fax: (01202) 740995. Email: writintl@globalnet.co.uk Website: www.worldwidewriters.com

Writers' News & Writing Magazine, Victoria House, 1st Floor, 143–145 The Headrow, Leeds LS1 5RL. Tel: (0113) 200 2929. Fax: (0013) 200 2928.
Email: derek.hudson@writersnews.co.uk
Website: www.writingmagazine.co.uk

Writers' News Home Study Division
Tel: (0113) 200 2929.
Email: rachel.bellerby@writersnews.co.uk
Website: www.writersnews.co.uk

Writers News Writing Competitions, Competitions & Awards Manager, Lorna Edwardson, PO Box 6055, Nairn IV12 4YB. Tel: (01667) 453351. Fax: (01667) 452365.
Email: dsjtcharitynairn@fsmail.net

Index